HONORING THE ANCESTORS
THE KEMETIC SHAMAN WAY:

A Practical Manual for Venerating and Working with the Ancestors from a God Perspective (Revised)

DERRIC MOORE

Copyright © 2019 Derric Moore.

All rights reserved. No part of this publication may be reproduced or transmitted in any form or by any means, electronic or mechanical, including photocopying, recording or by any information storage and retrieval system, without written permission from the author, except for the inclusion of brief quotations in a review. Includes selected bibliography and index.

Published by:
FOUR BROTHERS' PUBLICATIONS
P.O. Box 955
Leavenworth, KS 66048.

Cover art, artwork and illustrations by: Derric "Rau Khu" Moore
ISBN: 978-0-9855067-7-3
Printed in the United States of America

Dedication

To my loving wife and daughter,
thanks for your support and love.

To my nieces and nephew who made me stay up to 5 AM to talk about ancestors, spirits and spirituality.

To my ancestors and spirit guides,
whose shoulders I stand upon.

Table of Contents

Introduction: Why Another Book on Honoring the Ancestors? 1

Chapter 1: Surrendering to the Spirits 5

    Lessons from Papa, My Cuban Saint 5

    Called to Be a Shaman 9

    Lessons from the Spirits-Our Truest Teachers 12

    What Do Our Spirits Want? 16

    The Story of Osar 19

    Spirits Need Us as Much as We Need Them 22

    My Path, My Truth, My Salvation–Kamta Shamanism 24

Chapter 2: What are Spirit Guides? 29

    Someone Lied. Consciousness is Not Just in the Brain 29

    Are Spirits Real and Why Can't We All See Them? 32

    What Really Are Spirits? 35

    How to Contact Spirits 36

Chapter 3: Two Types of Spirits 41

    The Spirits Within 41

    The Spirits Without 43

Chapter 4: What and Who are Our Ancestors? 47

    How Do Our Ancestors Communicate with Us? 49

    How to See Your Spirits 51

    3 Reasons Why You Should Venerate Your Ancestors 51

    A Kemetic Theory on Reincarnation 54

    3 Rules to Follow to Venerate Your Ancestor Correctly 56

    Frequently Asked Questions About Honoring the Ancestors 59

Chapter 5: I Lost My Holy Ghost, but Found My Anointing 69

    Why is Kemet (Ancient Egypt) So Important? 75

    The Kamta Way 76

    The Netcharu: Guardian & Totem Spirits 79

    Aakhu: Ancestral Spirits and Spirit Guides 87

    The Aapepu: The Misguided and Confused Ancestral Spirits 102

    How to Build a Het Aakhu (Kemetic Shaman Ancestor Altar) 104

    Planning According to Divine Order 114

    Simple Technique to Contact Your Spirit Guide 115

    Got Bubbles in Your Glasses? 116

    What Do the Spirits Do With the Offerings? 117

    Additional Offerings 118

    Rituals with Spirit Money 120

    How to Divine with the Ancestor Altar 122

    When Will My Magick Work? 123

    Making A Way of Life 125

Final Words 128

Select Bibliography & Suggested Reading 129

Index 131

Photo Credits 132

Disclaimer

The information contained in this book is intended to be educational and should not be used for diagnosing, prescribing, or treating any health disorder whatsoever. This information should not replace consultation with a qualified healthcare professional. The content here is intended to be used as an adjunct to a rational and responsible healthcare program prescribed by a licensed healthcare practitioner.

This is a book about faith. As such, the author and publisher cannot guarantee the success any individual may achieve by using the exercises and techniques contained herein. Success and failure will vary. The author and publisher, therefore, are not liable for any misuse of the material contained herein.

To protect the identity and privacy of others, most of the names within this book have been adapted, modified and changed for confidentiality purposes. Any resemblance to actual persons, living or dead, is purely coincidental.

"The kingdom of heaven is within you, and whosoever shall know himself shall find it."

- Kemetic Proverb

Introduction:

Why Another Book on Honoring the Ancestors?

Far too often in North America, the "American way" has involved cultural appropriation, which usually results in perversion of very powerful and beautiful cultural practices into fads or trends, sometimes supersizing them into something worse. In my short years on the planet, I have seen this happen to so many cultural traditions and practices, leaving the original founders awestruck and speechless. The last bandwagon that everyone jumped on and "Americanized" was the Chinese tradition of Feng Shui. Now, the latest tradition to be supersized is ancestor veneration.

I am amazed by the number of books written about ancestor veneration, often portraying people who allegedly have been practicing it for years in this predominantly Protestant country, which tends to frown upon everything that is not "American." I know for a fact that much of the information published about ancestor veneration is simply repeated from cultural traditions that have honored their ancestors for centuries, developing both respect and reverence for the dead. As a result, a lot of what is published about venerating the ancestors is to introduce people to a religious practice. Consequently, ending up being a list of do's and don'ts, morphing this ancient, beloved and beautiful practice into yet another religion.

Allow me to be frank: if you are interested in ancestor veneration, it is likely because you have left or are considering leaving your organized religion for a certain reason. If I am correct, you do not want to adopt a tradition that imposes the same dogmatic religious beliefs you are trying to escape from, do you? At least, I didn't. That's why I wrote this book–to share with people how venerating my ancestors has helped me grow spiritually and become more enlightened.

What differentiates this book apart from others on this subject is that it is not written out of fear of the dead. Instead, it comes from the perspective that ancestors and spirits are not ghostly entities, but energies deserving of respect because we are them, and they are us.

To understand this perspective, we must set aside the Christian creation theory, which assumes that the Perfect Creator mistakenly made human beings who are flawed and imperfect, burdened for eternity by the Creator's supposed mistakes, often depicted as demons.

In contrast, the "Kemetic Creation Theory", teaches that in the beginning, there was nothing that existed, but a cosmic void known as Nyun, filled with hidden energy or Amun Ra. When the Almighty Divine Being realized Itself, it spoke itself into existence, causing the Ra (Visible Energy), to emerge from the dark cosmic void of Nyun. Finding no place to stand, the Almighty caused Maa (balance, law, order, truth, etc.) to ascend from Nyun, providing a foundation for the universe. Through Maa, the fiery, hot, and masculine Shu emerged, along with his polar opposite, the watery, cold, and feminine Tefnut. As a result of all of these complementary forces, the visible Ra (Energy) became KhepeRa (the Creative Energy) and Ra Atum (the Completed Energy, or simply the Energy of Change), eventually leading to the formation of matter over time.

Now, we must realize that the Kemetic Creation Theory is not merely a story about how the physical universe was created, but how we self-created ourselves as conscious Divine Beings. Here's the same creation theory retold in another way:

In our mother's womb, there was nothing but a cosmic void until life was called forth, which impregnated the egg. That life eventually grew, and nine months later, at birth, we became physical living beings.

Yes, you caused your own creation. You brought your own self into being. It was you that fought to be born, so you could take that first breath. You made yourself forget this so that you could have an authentic experience. If you remembered all of this, you would avoid all of the obstacles and pitfalls you intentionally set in your path to challenge your development into divinity. You made it so that you would be born into a society steeped in secular thinking—one that teaches you were made in the image of God, but you are flawed, sinned and powerless. To add insult to injury, you also chose to be born into a society where modern science trivializes every phenomenon as a product of chance.

But when you understand this theory, you know that you are a Divine Being who chose to be created, leading you to your conception. As a Divine Being with physical limitations, it makes sense that you would also call forth or assign yourself spiritual helpers—ancestors and spirit guides—to assist you in this incarnation.

Your ancestors, spirit guides, and guardian spirits are not superior to you; they serve you because that is their purpose. This means you are not meant to worship them, nor are they to worship you. Think of your spirits as extensions of your consciousness, but it is best to think of them as spiritual partners or allies.

Honoring the ancestors (and spirit guides) is a beautiful tradition and working with them can be fantastically empowering. However, to reach this spiritual stage with your spirits, you must stop looking to others for validation of your experiences and learn to trust your intuition. This is accomplished by understanding that what is right for you is what works for you, while what is wrong is what does not produce your desired results. It is simply trial and error. Since this book is based on my practical experience, it should be used as a guide to help you develop your own style. This is the reason I have aimed to write this manual in the simplest and easiest way possible to convey my message to you, the reader.

I want to express my gratitude for your purchase of this book. Without further ado, let's explore how to honor the ancestors from a Kemetic shamanistic perspective to enrich your life.

Chapter 1: Surrendering to the Spirits

Lessons from Papa, My Cuban Saint

When I first started honoring my ancestors, it was because I wanted to grow spiritually. The man who taught me the most about spirits was a little Cuban man whom I called Papa. Papa was a Babalawo (high priest) in the Lukumi religion, a member of the all-male Abakua Society, and a spiritist in the Espiritismo Cruzado (the Afro-Cuban Crossed Spiritism tradition). For those who haven't heard my story before, I became fascinated with all things Kemetic after the Holy Ghost failed to save me the way I'd hoped it would when I was a teenager.

You see, I was raised and brought up in the Pentecostal Church. My father was a preacher, and my mother was a songstress who was often invited all over the city of Detroit to sing. As a child, I never had any truly negative experiences with the Church, but everything changed when I became a teenager. Around this time, the crack cocaine epidemic was hitting Detroit hard in the mid-1980s, forcing me to question everything that I was taught about Christianity in order to survive the onslaught occurring in the streets. It was during this horrific time, my faith in Christianity and in God was challenged as I struggled to avoid drug-related violence and drug use, along with the other peer pressures that teenagers faced. When I turned to Christianity for answers, all the preachers told me and my friends to do was pray and give our lives to Jesus.

So, along with several of my friends, I went to the altar and pleaded for Jesus to save us and fill us with his Holy Ghost. I remember speaking in tongues, which was supposed to be proof that the Holy Ghost had descended upon me, but after a week or so, the feeling left. And it wasn't just me, it also left many of my friends as well, some of whom would lose their lives in the coming months.

We were left scared, frightened, and confused. My friends and I did what the preachers told us to do, to the best of our understanding, yet many of us still ended up in jail or, at worse, dead. Determined not to die, even though I kept finding myself in violent situations, I came to a realization: maybe God did not want me. It even seemed like God wanted Black people to suffer because the crack cocaine violence only affected people in the inner city, and not those in the suburbs around Detroit.

As time went by, I grew increasingly angry and disgusted because it felt like my fate was sealed as a young Black male. It was widely predicted throughout the city that young Black males would not live to see their 18th birthdays, and I was starting to believe the hype. The only protection I had was the Holy Ghost, which had left me. I became very defiant and self-destructive, even to the point of contemplating suicide. Fortunately, the Afrocentric Movement was growing in popularity, with numerous political awareness and conscious rap groups like Public Enemy, KRS-One and BDP, Poor Righteous Teachers, Brand Nubian, and X-Clan promoting awareness. This was when I met my first spirit guide, who gave me some clarity and encouraged me to learn about Ancient Egypt.

I survived the late 1980s and early 1990s by immersing my time and energy in reading, studying, and learning about the Ancient Egyptians–Kemetic people, their history, and religion. In the process, my disdain for Christianity grew stronger, as it had failed to help me. Later, I would learn that the reason Christianity didn't work for me was because I'd never officially been taught how to truly pray or empower myself, which explained why my friends and I became vulnerable to evil forces. When I found out that much of the Christian beliefs and practices were borrowed or outright stolen from Kemet, and that these versions of Kemetic practices were often poor manifestations of the Kemetic religion–it all made sense. Christianity was not empowering people because it was not designed to do so; it was a religion repurposed by slave owners to maintain social control. In other words, Christianity was not spiritual, which explained the lack of empowerment. I saw the church as an institution where financial abuse, corruption, widespread pedophilia, molestation, and hypocrisy ran rampant among church officials, Yes, the church is man-made consisting of man-made rules, which many people were breaking, and at same time all under the guise of God's authority. In my mind, the reason people were breaking these "rules" was that God was absent from most churches, which had become Sunday places of fellowship, socializing, not spiritual empowerment.

Like so many others, I simply threw the baby out with the bathwater, so to speak. I continued reading and studying everything I could about Kemet, realizing that the power of the Kemetic society stemmed from their religion, which blanketed their entire way of life. I absorbed all the Kemetic legends and myths that I could find, but when I tried to implement the Kemetic religion in my life, I got very confused.

So, I joined various study groups and collaborated with these individuals, but still, I didn't make any progress. I put myself under the tutelage of an individual who claimed to be a priestess, only to be taken advantage of both spiritually and financially. I remember feeling so disgusted and ready to turn my back on this whole "spirituality thang" that I said, "Spirituality should not have to be this hard." A few days later, I met Papa.

Papa taught me a lot of things. He shared stories about his life in Cuba, his mixed feelings about Fidel Castro, how he along with other Cubans were sent to Africa to help fight for African independence. He also talked about how he and other Cuban refugees were treated when they first arrived in the United States and encountered the Ku Klux Klan. He said it was at that very moment he understood, on a personal level, what it was like to be Black in America.

I enjoyed talking to Papa because he was a wise old man, and he gave me a broader perspective on what it meant to be Black outside of the lens of American racism. One day, while visiting him, I was going on and on about what I learned about the Kemetic people and how great they were. He interrupted me and said, "But you don't live there now."

Papa went on to say that while the Kemetic people had built an incredible society, what they did back then could not directly help me now because we live in different times. It was at that moment; I think he realized that I had been mimicking the Kemetic culture. He advised me to focus on the concepts and principles, because this form the roots of all African societies. Papa explained to me that this was why the African religions in Cuba had evolved to be different from how it is practiced in Africa. If these African religions had stayed the same in the Americas, as they were in Africa, they would have become obsolete because they were not suited for the challenges of the new world.

Papa helped me to realize that we, as African Americans, never really had a chance to develop our own spirituality because we were constantly living under the threat of the dominant culture. He told me that many of us chase after other peoples' spirituality instead of simply looking at what has been directly right in front of our faces the whole time. Not too long after this conversation, I lost contact with Papa, as if he had only miraculously come into my life to deliver to me a few messages and then mysteriously departed.

This whole spiritual quest experience made me upset, and after more than ten years of what felt like a constant uphill battle just to find my spiritual path,. I was exhausted. I was tired of trying to be spiritual, tired of trying to learn about spirituality. So, I stopped and decided to focus on making money instead.

Called to Be a Shaman

Having spent so much time chasing after the dream of becoming more spiritual, I decided it was time to shift my focus and pursue a career. Prior to getting on this whole spiritual path, my goal had been to become an engineer. After practicing mathematics for so many years, it has become one of my favorite subjects along with the sciences. So, I thought the quickest way to start making some serious money was to finish my college degree and find engineer-related jobs.

It didn't take long for me to finish my undergraduate degree since I only needed a few more credits. Right after I graduated, I got a job working as a laboratory technician. Around that time, I met an Oshun priestess. After talking to her for a while, she told me, "You were called to be a shaman," and said I needed to heed this calling. This priestess, whom I had come to call Iya (which means "Mother" in Yoruba), explained to me that the reason I was having so many problems was because my calling was to be a shaman. Unlike other paths, though, she told me that no one could actually sit down and have a formal one-to-one training session with me. Instead, I had to learn directly from the Spirits. Then, Iya told me that, because most Christians are not familiar with spiritual traditions, they interpret a calling like mine as being called to the pulpit–to be a preacher. But Iya clarified that I was not called to be a preacher; I was called to be a shaman.

Iya gave me a list of books to read to learn more about shamanism, but I did not want to be a shaman. In all of the movies I'd seen, shamans had a hard time–they often ended up seriously messed up. So, I read a few of the books that she recommended but chose to ignore the calling.

Then, one day my health began deteriorating. I had wanted to lose weight, but I lost almost 50 lbs. in just a matter of weeks. I hated my job, couldn't stand my coworkers, and my relationships were falling apart. Suddenly, I did not have any money left on me. The next thing I knew, I got walking pneumonia and struggled to breathe. Although it took me a long time to really understand what Papa was telling me, it finally dawned on me while I was lying on the hospital gurney several years later.

As I lay there, contemplating if I was going to die or not, I cried out (in my inner voice) and said, I tried to do what I thought was best, but I'm tired, and I'm giving up. That's when it became apparent that the reason, I was in the condition I was in was a result of doing what "I" thought was best, and not what the Spirit knew was best for me.

Then, my ancestors and spirit guides visited me, and that was when I understood what Papa was telling me: culture is not static; but dynamic. Papa was trying his best to tell me that I did not live in ancient Kemet, which was an agrarian society ruled by a spiritual minded ruler and a priesthood. Instead, I lived in the United States, a society structured by racism and fascism, where spirituality is often discouraged and places great emphasis on self-interest. I needed a type of spirituality that didn't exist in ancient Kemet but was based on similar concepts and principles.

What I failed to realize was that the Kemetic people were able to develop a highly spiritual culture because they lived in an environment that was conducive for them to do so. The Kemetic society was wealthy due to the inundation of the Nile River. They did not have to worry about food and shelter like we do today. They did not have to worry about racism. The most they had to worry about was occasional border skirmishes. With little to no worries, they were able to focus on contemplating the mysteries. We do not live in those times today.

You see, prior to the advent of the transatlantic slave trade in Africa, most African religions were more focused on enlightenment, since the culture of the people were more spiritually oriented. This was not the case in the Americas. Here, the dominant European culture was only focused on capitalizing and exploiting all the resources by any means necessary. The Africans who were abducted, enslaved, and taken to these territories had to focus on survival and maintaining their way of life. Consequently, the African religions in the Americas became more aggressive, designed to assist adherents survive in a hostile environment. Papa told me that this was the reason why Santeria (or Lukumi) differs from the Yoruba religion practiced in Nigeria; it had to adapt to an Afro-Latino cultural context, in order to help the African descendants, survive in a new world. The same adaptation had to be done in North America, which meant I had to start applying the Kemetic concepts and principles in a more aggressive manner.

After coming to this realization, I felt I could relate better to the first Africans brought to this country. So, I humbled myself and asked my Spirits to show me what I needed to know to heal my whole self. When I was discharged from the hospital, I returned home and rebuilt my ancestor altar. This time, instead of following and mimicking what others had done, I simply followed my intuition, and allowed my ancestors and spirit guides to speak to me directly.

Lessons from the Spirits-Our Truest Teachers

When I first allowed my Spirits to direct me, I remember stating to them that we (Africans in America) had lost our culture, so I did not understand how we could create a religion as was done in Cuba. They showed me that what Africans practiced in North America became what people today call Conjure or Rootwork. Conjure or Rootwork was not all about doing spell work as it is touted today. It was practiced differently from individual to individual because Africans had different cultural perspectives. The basis of most Conjure or Rootwork traditions was Kongo Angolan, because they were the first Africans brought to North America. The descendants of the Kongo-Angolan region brought with them their BaSimbi, BaKulu, and BaNkyu. As a result, Conjure or Rootwork had a very strong spiritual component. But because Africans and their descendants were considered to be "property" and viewed as not having a culture, our ancestors took what they brought from Africa and blended it with Christianity, creating a new religion in this unfamiliar land.

Contrary to popular belief, Hoodoo has more to do with working with ancestors than many people realize. Now, I don't care what the scholars say, but Hoodoo was not the name my ancestors called their faith. In fact, no one in my family or anyone I have come in contact with Hoodoo-practicing ancestors called it as such. Hoodoo was considered witchcraft, and, to most traditional African minds, witchcraft was considered evil because it is the practice of magical arts for selfish reasons. However, Europeans did not understand the difference, so they called everything "Hoodoo."

Hoodoo is actually a distortion of the religious term "Vodou" and the derogatory term "Voodoo." Folklorist E.O. Ballard offers the best explanation, suggesting that "Hoodoo" comes from the Spanish word Judio (pronounced hoo-dy-oh), meaning "Jewish." It refers to Africans who, like many of the Jews, after hearing the Gospel of Christ, refused to convert to Christianity and continued to instead practice Judaism or Old Testament ways as opposed to the New Testament. Ballard cited proof of this theory in Cuba, where practitioners of the Congo faith Palo Mayombe practiced a path called Palo Judio, which means "Jewish Palo" or a spiritual path free from Christian influences or iconography. This explanation makes a lot of sense to me since Conjure and Rootwork are deeply influenced by Kongo traditions.

Our ancestors, who had no real homes and were often forced to live in shacks, faced regular abuse and were treated worse than animals. They were unable to fully develop Conjure or Rootwork, so they practiced it in hush harbors, fields, and groves until they were able to adapt and modify it for practicing it in plain sight alongside their unsuspecting "Christian" oppressors. To do this, they syncretized their spiritual beliefs with biblical characters, which helped them identify with the biblical Children of Israel and see the greatest conjure man or rootworker as Moses.

My Spirits basically revealed to me that it is a myth that African Americans lost their culture. What was lost was the philosophy and theology behind the culture, which they told me was linked to the dikenga dia Kongo or tendwa kia nza-n' Kongo) also known as the yowa or Kongo Cross.

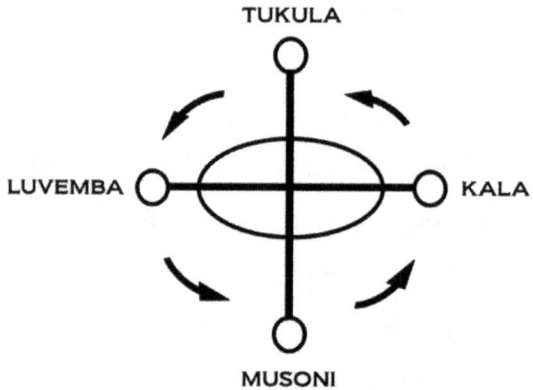

The Kongo Cross was foundational to Kongo-Angolan culture and permeated every aspect of the Old Kongo-Angolan society. When the first Africans were brought to North America, they were either Christians or already familiar with Christianity, as the Kongo monarchy had declared it the official religion prior to the advent of the slave trade. Consequently, most of the Kongo-Angolan people had a working syncretism between their traditional beliefs and practices and the Christian faith. So, when they arrived on the shores of North America, the Kongo Cross came with them and became the main guide used for self-initiation, which followed the **Rule of the Sun**.

To understand what the Rule of the Sun initiation was, we must understand that initiation means there is no going back after the experience. Once you pass the first grade in school, generally speaking, you cannot go back to kindergarten. Once you have had sex the first time, you cannot go back and reclaim your virginity. So, there are two types of initiation: one where you're formally initiated through a rite of passage or ceremony, and one where an individual is initiated into a new experience automatically by life, such as puberty, adulthood, or psychic experiences, etc. The Rule of the Sun initiation followed this second form of initiation, and this is how the Kongo Cross survived slavery.

Eventually, the philosophy and theology behind the Kongo Cross was lost in North America because it was syncretized with biblical stories like the Wall of Jericho, which resulted in the loss of its true meaning. I remember wondering if I could go to the Democratic Republic of the Congo to relearn the Kongo philosophy from the surviving priests and priestesses, as many African Americans have done by returning to Nigeria to reclaim the Yoruba faith. But I was quickly reminded that this was impossible; the Kongo-Angolan region was severely affected by the slave trade, its people were devastated by the Europeans, and today the region is still ravaged with the effects of former colonial influences and civil war.

Then, my ancestors reminded me that the Kemetic Ra was not a sun god but was more like the Jewish El, where "El" is an attribute of the Creator. Through making one to one correspondence between the Kongo Cross and the various names of the Kemetic Ra, I discovered a cultural connection between the

Kongo and Kemetic people, which led to the creation of the Maa Aankh cosmogram.

What Do Our Spirits Want?

The Maa Aankh is composed of two Kemetic words: Maa, meaning "balance, law, truth, righteousness, order, etc.," and Aankh, which means "life, to live, and to swear an oath." Thus, Maa Aankh translates "to live righteously," "righteous living," and/or "to swear an oath to be Maa."

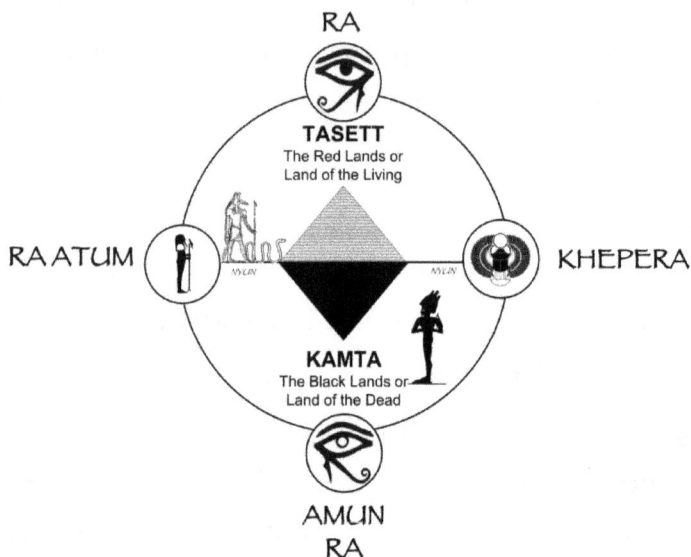

The basic understanding of the Maa Aankh is that our world consists of two realities: a physical realm above, where we the living dwell, called TASETT (the Red Lands or Land of the Living), and a spiritual realm below, where the spirits reside, called KAMTA (the Black Lands or Land of the Dead).

Surrounding KAMTA and TASETT are four discs that represent the four stages of the sun and the evolution of our soul (Kemetic/KiKongo/English):

- Khepera/Kala - Sunrise: the Moment of Birth
- Ra/TuKula - Midday: the Moment of Life

- Ra Atum/Luvemba - Sunset: the Moment of Death (or Change)
- Amun Ra/Musoni - Midnight (when the sun shines on the other side): – the Moment of Rebirth.

To go into the full explanation of the Four Ras of the Maa Aankh here would take us beyond the scope of this book but, from a shamanic healing perspective, the four moments of the sun, or the Four Ras represent the four stages leading to true spiritual empowerment. Initiation into the Four Ras of the Maa Aankh begins with:

1. **Ra Atum Initiation or the Moment of Death**, symbolized by the setting sun, which indicates that whenever we experience great loss, misfortune, problems, obstacles, setbacks, illness, etc., it is because there is an imbalance within our soul.

2. **Amun Ra Initiation or the Moment of Rebirth**, symbolized by the midnight moon, is the moment of reflections. It is in this moment, when we humble ourselves and learn to go within, that messages are revealed to us from our spirits.

3. **Khepera Initiation or the Moment of Birth**, symbolized by the rising sun, marks the beginning of a new individual. At the Khepera moment, after the spirits reveal the truth to us, we are expected to begin practicing living.

4. **Ra Initiation or the Moment of Life**, symbolized by the midday sun, indicates a moment of growth at a cosmic crossroad. This is the moment in our life when we must fight for what we want or the truth we want to live. It is here that we face our inner demons, because it is at this moment we are going to be judged, challenged, and tested. At

this stage, we are presented with an opportunity to either grow or risk returning to our old ways. If we fail this test, like the setting sun, we fall back to the Ra Atum moment and are given another opportunity to do it again. If we pass, we are allowed to move to the next level, assist others facing similar ills, while enjoying the rewards of successfully completing a Maa Aankh. An individual who has successfully completed the Maa Aankh in regard to a particular situation is a Maa Kheru, which literally means in Kemetic, "true of voice," which simply means "born again."

This understanding helped me realize that when an individual repeatedly faces the same problems, it is often because they have not yet passed the Ra Initiation stage. This perspective made me realize that my illness was an initiation.

Since I did not have any spiritual teachers around me, I wondered how I could be initiated, because I still believed I needed to undergo a formal initiation. That's when my Spirits inspired me to read the *Story of Osar* from a new understanding.

The Story of Osar

According to legend, when Osar (Osiris) came into power, his people were in constant war with one another. Then, Osar discovered the sacred teachings of Maa, which helped people govern themselves and live with one another peacefully. Osar traveled all over the country spreading these teachings and taught the people the science of agriculture, which he had learned from his wife, Oset (Isis). Consequently, almost overnight, the Kemetic people ceased fighting with one another, uniting Kemet into one country. Then, the Kemetic discovery of agriculture transformed Kemet into a very prosperous nation.

Now, everyone loved and was grateful for what Osar had done–except for his youngest brother Set, who was so full of jealousy and plotted to kill Osar. One day, after Osar returned home from spreading his teachings around the world, Set planned a celebration in Osar's honor. During the celebration, when Osar had consumed a lot of ale and was drunk, Set and his 72 conspirators[1] tricked Osar into lying inside a chest. Then, they rose up, soldered the chest shut, and threw it in the Nile, thus killing the first king of Kemet.

---

[1] The 72 conspirators of Set correspond to the 72 Goetia demons that the biblical King Solomon captured.

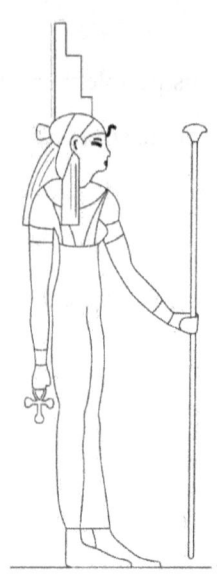

When Oset, who had not attended the celebration held in Osar's honor, heard what Set had done to her beloved husband, she put on her mourning clothes and went in search of the chest. Ra, having pity upon Oset, sent her Npu (Anubis) to assist in the search. They discovered that a tree had grown around the chest. After asking the ruler of the foreign land where it was found to cut down the tree and give her the chest, Oset, completely overcome with grief, opened the chest and magically conceived a true heir of Osar.

When Oset left to give birth to Hru-sa-oset (Hru, son of Oset) or simply Hru, she hid the chest containing Osar's body in the marshes. However, during a hunting expedition, Set found the chest. In a fit of rage, he hacked Osar's corpse into 14 pieces and scattered them throughout the country. Once again, when Oset learned what Set had done, she searched for the body parts of Osar with Npu, this time joined by her younger sister, Nebthet, who was also Set's wife  and was appalled by his actions. Together, they collected the body parts and performed the proper burial ceremony with the help of Djahuti (Thoth), so that Osar could rest.

When Hru came of age, he challenged his uncle Set for the throne. But Set, being older and more experienced in warfare than his nephew, managed to defeat Hru on the battlefield. In one epic battle, Set managed to get close enough to gouge out the young prince's eye, forcing Hru to retreat. To heal his eye, Hru fled to see his father's old vizier and friend Djahuti who restored the young prince's eye perfectly.

The next time Hru met Set on the battlefield, he defeated Set's army and even managed to cut Set's gonads. However, despite his defeat, Set refused to yield. Instead, he launched a propaganda campaign, claiming that Hru was not the legitimate heir of Osar. The campaign garnered so much attention that eventually the matter was taken to court and put into the hands of a tribunal to decide who should be the rightful ruler of Kemet.

Because Set continued to have influence over the courts, the legal case deliberated for days, possibly even months, until finally, Djahuti decided to call upon Osar from beyond the grave. Osar, appearing as Tem, spoke to the tribunal and confirmed that Hru was indeed his rightful heir, and that Set was lying. He reminded the tribunal that he had been the first king to unify Kemet by teaching the people Maa (righteousness). Osar explained that Maa, which reflects the life that we live in death, had made him the Lord of Underworld. He urged the tribunal to judge righteously–in other words, to do what is right

rather than–warning them that he would judge them accordingly in the afterlife.

Upon hearing the testimony of Osar, the tribunal ruled in Hru's favor, and awarded him the double Pschent crown of Kemet. As for Set, his punishment was to become the wind of Osar, meaning the one responsible for confessing all of the evil he had done in order to promote the goodness of the teachings of Osar.

Spirits Need Us as Much as We Need Them

I had to change my beliefs. With this new insight and understanding about Spirits, I began to see that, contrary to my Christian upbringing, which taught me to fear the unknown, I had come to understand that spirits are not more powerful than us, living human beings. Spirits are unique because they do not have physical bodies and, therefore, are not bound by time and space. This means all spirits have the ability to travel all around the world in a matter of seconds and see beyond our physical means, which is the reason they are often called upon for insight into the future. They can walk through solid matter like walls and influence how people think, but their lack of a physical body prevents them from experiencing life as we know it.

Spirits are unable to experience the pleasure of food, smell, taste, touch, or even experience sex. They can, however, partake in the essence of certain things, but to do so, they need our participation.

Because we, the living, are inside physical bodies, we are bound by time and space, which gives us the ability to experience life. However, it prevents us from seeing beyond our physical limits, so we are restricted to the present moment and immediate surroundings.

Partnering with spirits allows us to "expand our awareness" because we gain the ability to see past, present and future events. Spirits, on the other hand, can experience life indirectly and directly through us, which is vital for their development. Hence, the saying: **"Spirits need us, as much as we need them."** Neither is superior to the other; it is a partnership of equal exchange. If a spirit feels that you cannot provide what it needs, then it will not enter into a partnership with you. At the same time, if you feel that a spirit cannot offer you anything of value, then you are not by any means obligated to work with or stay in a relationship with that spirit. The relationship between you and the spirit is a mutually beneficial one, where you care for the spirit, and the spirit will care for you–and vice versa. This relationship is reflected between Hru and Osar in the *Story of Osar*.

Understand this: **without the Living, there would be no Spirits; but without the Spirits, there would be no Living**. This is the primary purpose for venerating and working with your Ancestors, Spirit Guides, and Guardian Spirits.

However, to work effectively with spirits requires that we develop self-discipline and spiritual development. Self-discipline is simply combating your habits and vices, while spiritual development is the result of recognizing your mistakes and making a conscious effort to never repeat them ever again. Failure to use both provides fertile ground for our insecurities, fears and negative thoughts to manifest and become a physical reality, thus feeding our ego-self, or Set. Therefore, we must wage war against our lower self, our Set.

My Path, My Truth, My Salvation–Kamta Shamanism

This realization made me see that the Kemetic people never worshipped their Ancestors or any Spirit for that matter; they venerated them. And the reason I went through this entire ordeal was to be initiated back into this truth. Upon realizing that I had just been self-initiated, I now understood that shamans in ancient times were spiritual scientists, basically men or women who studied and practiced spiritual psychology. Yes, shamans go into trance to find answers, but it is so that they can understand a particular spirit associated with a human behavior.

After I came to grips with what a shaman was, thanks to my ancestors' assistance and my spirit guides patiently answering my questions, I finally found clarity, peace of mind, and an understanding of my purpose. When I read the *Story of Osar* this time, it made me immediately realize that the Creator or Supreme Being was not necessarily absent when Set killed his brother, just like the God in the Bible was not absent when Cain killed Abel. The Creator, the Supreme Being, or whatever you choose to call the Divine, simply did not and does not get involved. Thus, the reason evil exists is because it is necessary and serves a divine purpose as one of the sides of a two-sided coin. Simply put, if evil did not exist, neither would good, because you cannot have one without the other, like darkness and light, water and fire, etc.

Therefore, good and evil, technically speaking, do not exist because what is considered good from one person's perspective may be seen as evil from another's viewpoint. A prime example of this is slavery, which clearly shows that the Creator, the Supreme Being, the Universe, God, etc., does not pick sides between good and evil. This is the same reason why the same air that fills our lungs also filled the lungs of Hitler, Mussolini, and other so-called "evil" people.

Evil, according to the Maa Aankh, is simply imbalance (isfet), whereas good is balance (maa). In the *Story of Osar*, Set symbolizes our lower self, which is responsible for physical survival, instincts, desires, vitality, and all things related to the physical body and ego. Meanwhile, Osar symbolizes our Higher Self and enlightened ancestral spirits, which is responsible for our eternal connection to the infinite Universe. Both Osar and Set represent imbalance when relied solely upon for salvation. Balance is achieved through Hru, who symbolizes the conscious mind integrating both the Higher and the lower selves–Osar and Set–working together.

So, the Creator, the Supreme Being, the Universe, God, etc., is not responsible for our salvation…we are. Life does not happen to us but for us.

This realization meant that my illness was not a curse. It was a sign that I was living in an imbalance state (disconnected from my Higher Self or Osar), which manifested as a physical illness. It became evident that to achieve a balanced state, I had to, psychologically speaking, align my lower self with my Higher Self by declaring what I wanted and allowing the Higher Self to resolve the issue. Ritualistically, this involved working with my Spirits and, metaphorically speaking, resurrecting my Osar, much like how Hru defeated Set.

As a result, I tested my theory, and now, over a decade later, I can testify to its effectiveness. This spiritual system is what I call *Kamta Shamanism*.

Although the term shaman comes from the Tungus tribe in Siberia, where it means "one who sees in the dark" or "spiritual healer," it has been used by anthropologists and laypeople alike to describe magicians, witch doctors, psychics, healers, reiki specialists, diviners, tribal priests, etc. A shaman, technically speaking, is a man or woman who focuses on maintaining and restoring balance–between people, between people and Nature (plants, animals, etc.), between people and spirits, and within individuals' minds and bodies. Hence, a shaman is different from all other psychic and spiritual practitioners in the sense that they are healers who have altered their consciousness to go to the other side and retrieve solutions to fix problems or restore balance.

Therefore, shamanism is a way of life, which consists of altering one's consciousness to access the other side and retrieve solutions to fix problems or restore balance daily. Simply put, shamanism is a practice of direct revelation from working with helping spirits.

Kamta Shamanism is direct revelation from working with our ancestors and spirit guides using Kemetic theology and the remnants of the Kongo-Angolan philosophy that survived slavery in North America. Since most African American are the descendants of the Kongo, BaKuba, Bantu, Akan, Igbo, Fula, Yoruba and Mandika with varying amounts of Native American and European ancestry, the Kemetic *Story of Osar* has a more profound meaning and symbolizes the clans setting aside their differences and uniting for a common goal, which is freedom and liberation for the people. Therefore, in Kamta Shamanism, there is no one individual or shaman responsible for keeping balance; from an Osarian perspective, it is the responsibility of all adults within the community to keep and maintain balance and harmony in their families, homes, and communities. Kamta Shamanism relies on:

- Communicating regularly with the ancestors and spirit guides
- Working with the spirits of the dead outside of one's biological and cultural circle to perform magickal rites
- Setting lights to elevate spirits
- Spiritual development by learning self-discipline, patience, humility, commitment, wisdom and persistence

These are all practices and skills that many of us would have developed had slavery not occurred because they are seen as our natural birthright. Understand that, from an Osarian perspective, we are all spiritual beings with a soul inside a physical body. We were not meant to suffer; the only reason we do is because we live in a Setian-influenced society and have all been tricked into believing that we are powerless, downtrodden, and sinful beings, which contradicts the belief that the Supreme Being is Perfect. As a result, the Divine Spark within us all, symbolized as Osar, sleeps within.

Magick is part of our birthright, and through practice, anyone can awaken the Divine Spark, or Osar, within and use it to heal themselves and others. We must replace the belief that we are sinned human beings born from an imperfect creation called Adam and Eve with the understanding that we are all Children of Osar, each with a sleeping giant within waiting to be awakened.

In this book, I will discuss how to hone these techniques and apply them by discussing the basics of honoring the ancestors, as well as the more advanced aspects of incorporating them into every aspect of our lives. Our Spirits are around us all the time, offering insights on how to enhance and enrich our lives, whether it's a hunch to avoid entering a relationship with certain people because it is counterproductive, or simply having a conversation with an individual at the grocery store to improve your business.

They are our first line of defense and the first entities we need to learn how to work with to develop spiritually.

Chapter 2: What are Spirit Guides?

Someone Lied. Consciousness is Not Just in the Brain

The billion-dollar question that most people want an answer to is, "Are spirits real?" The answer to this question is not a clear cut yes or no. Based on my research and experimentation on this subject, I believe that spirits (angels, demons, or whatever people choose to call them) are indeed real and not just figments of our imagination. However, from my experience with spirits, I've also come to believe that our minds use our imagination to make spirits manifest themselves through evocation or invocation.

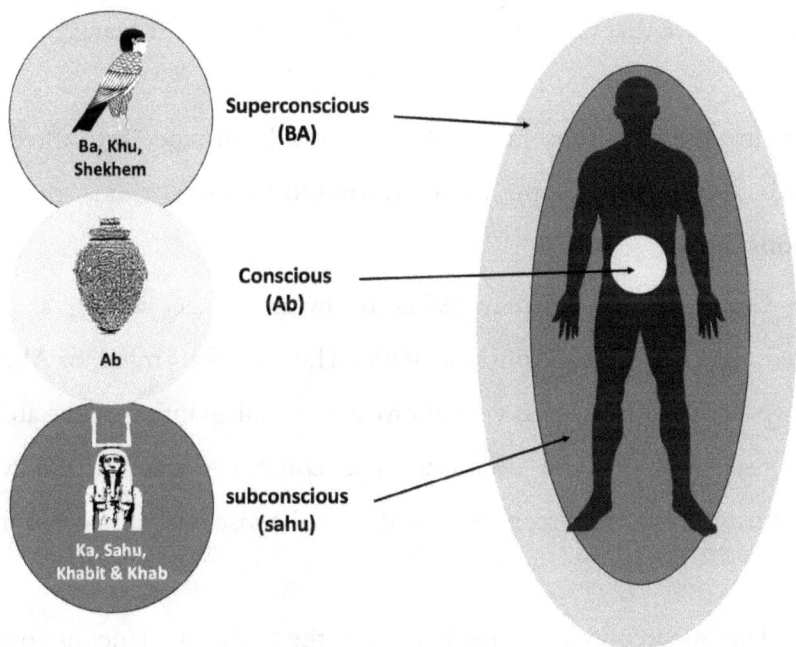

To understand this, we must understand that consciousness is not just a small aspect confined to our brain. Instead, consciousness incorporates our entire being and is best understood as a multi-layered organism with a host of systems, similar to how our physical body has numerous systems (e.g., nervous system, skeletal system, digestive system, muscular system, etc.). Think about how your body grows, digests food, and assimilates cells without you even thinking about it. This is proof of an organized system at work. The Kemetic (Ancient Egyptian) sages were among the first cultures to map out this consciousness, referring to it as the **ba, khu, shekhem, ren, ab, ka, sahu, khabit,** and **khab**.

Unfortunately, archeologists and egyptologists (intentionally lowercased) who were unfamiliar with ancient African thinking, particularly ancestor veneration, reincarnation, and spiritual development, misunderstood and misinterpreted these concepts. They mistakenly labeled them as divisions of the soul, leading people to believe that consciousness resides only within our being.

So, for simplicity's purpose, these divisions can be grouped into three parts: the **Ab (conscious)**, the **BA (Superconscious)**, and the **sahu (subconscious)**.

- Consciousness typically refers to living in the waking state and interacting with the physical world. The conscious mind, or **Ab**, is the part of our being that we refer to as our soul, granting us the ability to make choices and decisions. The conscious mind is sandwiched between the Superconscious and the subconscious parts of our being.

- The Superconscious, also known as the Collective Unconsciousness, Higher Self, or BA, corresponds to our neocortex. It is the creative, intuitive, all-knowing, and all-powerful part of our being. Suddenly, answers that seem to come out-of-the-blue are all credited to the Superconscious, something that great geniuses and inventors attribute their creations to. As for where these intuitive ideas or memories come from, Swiss psychiatrist C. G. Jung theorizes that they are the memories of our ancestral past. Jung states in The Archetypes and the Collective Unconscious (1968):

"We could therefore say that every mother contains her daughter in herself and every daughter her mother, and that every woman extends backwards into her mother and forward into her daughter. This participation and intermingling give rise to that peculiar uncertainty as regards time... The conscious experience of these ties produces the feeling that her life is spread out over generations – the first step toward the immediate experience and conviction of being outside time, which brings a feeling of immortality. The individual's life is elevated into a type; indeed, it becomes the archetype...This leads to restoration...of the lives of her ancestors, who now through the bridge of the momentary individual, pass down into the generations of the future."

In other words, our ancestors and their memories are all within us, something Jung initially referred to as racial consciousness. Spirits exist in the great unknown of our mind.

- The subconscious, or **sahu**, is the lower self, corresponding to our hindbrain (also called the reptilian brain or R-complex). it is the most primitive and the oldest part of our being. The subconscious governs all of our automatic bodily functions that occur without us thinking, such as breathing, digestion, etc. This part of our mind focuses solely on our physical survival. Everything that you have learned from your parents, friends, schools, religious leaders, and society was meant to help you physically survive.

The four divisions of the subconscious, known as the ka, sahu, khabit, and khab, all correspond to the emotional, lower astral, upper astral, and mental realms, respectively. These four divisions are always sending us messages, and they have an effect on our day-to-day lives. For this reason, they are called the lower-self, ego-self, or the Ego.

It should be noted that everything that exists from this perspective is Conscious. Plants, animals, minerals, crystals, etc. all possess consciousness. However, what distinguishes other beings from human beings is that we have an Ab (Conscious Mind/Heart/Soul).

Therefore, we are surrounded by conscious beings or spirits. All Higher spirits tend to communicate with us through the intuition of our BA (Superconscious). Lower spirits communicate with us through the emotions of the subconscious (sahu), while benevolent spirits (such as ancestors and spirit guides) tend to communicate with us intellectually through the Ab (conscious).

Are Spirits Real and Why Can't We All See Them?

Spirits communicate with us all the time because they exist within our subconscious on the mental plane, which is the highest level of the subconscious mind. This is where the seeds of our conscious desires are sown. So when we want to accomplish a task, our ancestral spirits and spirit guides – also called our angels – appear to give us insight on how to achieve that task at hand. However, the reason most of the messages from the Spirits go unnoticed is that people live their day-to-day life in what is called the beta state of trance.

Trance, for the record, is basically a state of awareness that we all enter into, where we are either semi-responsive to external stimuli or unresponsive all together. Most research on the subject indicates that there are four basic trance states that our mind enters: beta, alpha, theta, and delta.

- **Beta** - This is the normal waking trance state we use to function daily in our life. When we are in the Beta trance state, our brain waves range from 14 to 40 cycles per second, indicating that the mind is highly active. In Beta, we are talking, debating, teaching, etc. It is basically a closed-mind state where we have preconceived ideas about what is possible and what isn't.

- **Alpha** – A more relaxed state of awareness. In the Alpha trance state, our brain waves range from 7 to 14 cycles per second. Alpha occurs naturally whenever we are taking a casual walk, have just had a pleasurable sexual experience, relax after consuming alcohol, driving for long periods of time, listening to a boring lecturer, or just before we fall asleep or wake up (what is called twilight.) Basically, anytime our mind and body are relaxed, where we are lucid and reflective, we are in Alpha state. When you are in Alpha, you are less critical, less anxious, and calmer. You have a better memory and are able to make better decisions because you are more focused.

- **Theta** – A deeper relaxed state of awareness than Alpha. In Theta, brain waves range from 4 to 7 cycles per second. You might enter

Theta when you drive for long periods of time and find yourself falling asleep at the wheel because the repetitiveness of doing small moves and seeing dashed lines on the road has put you into this trance. Theta is our dream state or where REM (Rapid Eye Movement) sleep occurs. It is also where drowsiness and deeper forms of daydreaming or lucid dreaming occurs, meaning you are aware that you are dreaming. Researchers have found from observing yoga masters that theta is associated with creativity, super learning, self-reprogramming, spiritual experiences, and deep meditation. In fact, it's the reason why most kids are so imaginative and open-minded, as they are not afraid to try new things, making them "little sponges" of new information because they spend a lot of time in theta. This is why kids have no problem pretending to be someone else and can easily learn new material.

- **Delta** – A very relaxed state of awareness. When we enter into Delta, brain waves range from 1.5 and 4 cycles per second. It never goes to zero because that would mean that we are brain dead. Delta is where deep non-REM (Rapid Eye Movement), or dreamless sleep occurs. I like to think of Delta as the state where we sleep so deeply that we don't even move.

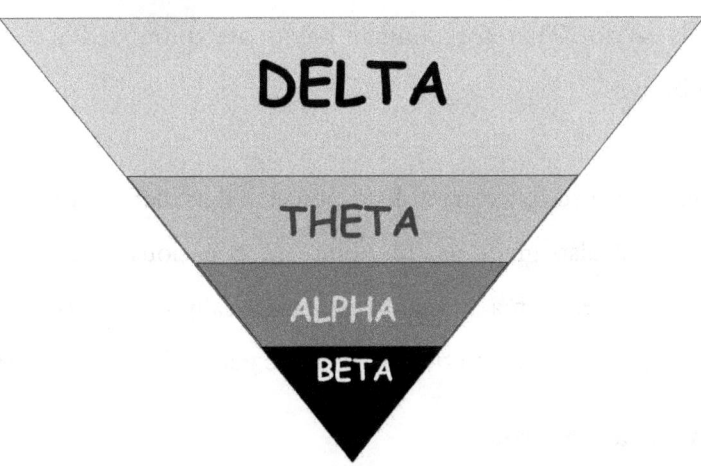

What this means is that I believe spirits exist. But if someone who's not familiar with magickal or spiritual practices saw me talking to one of my spirits, they would not see the spirit as I do. Instead, they would simply see me talking to myself because they are still in the Beta state of trance, whereas I have entered into Alpha or some other higher trance state. This, in my opinion, explains why hard-nosed, Western-trained scientists can never prove the existence of spirits, because they are in the Beta mind state.

What Really Are Spirits?

I define a spirit as an invisible, intelligent, and conscious energy. From a shamanic perspective, everything that exists around us is a spirit existing inhabiting a physical body. Plants and animals are spirits. You and I are spiritual beings within a physical vehicle that we commonly call the body.

In case you are wondering, the difference between human beings and all of the other spiritual beings is that we have an eternal soul, which gives us the ability to make choices and decisions, as well as perceive beyond our physical awareness. An example of our soul's prowess can be seen in the fact that human beings bury their dead and perform rest-in-peace rituals, whereas plants and animals do not. Therefore, human beings are spirits with a soul inside of a physical body.

Because we have a soul, we are able to perceive that there is life after physical death. Our soul also gives us the ability to consciously reason and make decisions. So, whenever a human being physically dies, it is the soul that survives the whole death experience—what we generally refer to as spirit.

How to Contact Spirits

Most shamanic and magickal traditions are rooted in getting help from spirits of some kind because all spirits can be asked, ordered, or persuaded to assist. All that is required is knowing which type of spirit you are dealing with and how to approach them. For instance, you would not ask spirits of love to banish your noisy neighbors, nor would you ask mothering spirits to help you seek justice. Spirits each have a realm of influence they belong to, so when you call upon one to assist you, you are no longer relying solely on yourself but instead receiving ideas, thoughts, and energy from a spirit.

The key to contacting a spirit is that you must believe they are real. When you truly believe in the existence of spirits, you can validate all of the paranormal experiences you might or will have to them, such as feeling your hair stand on the back of your neck, sensing a presence of an entity, hearing noises and/or whispers, etc. All of the weird experiences you will feel can be attributed to them, which will stimulate your emotions and help you get what you want. Therefore, if you feel strange or unsettled after contacting spirits, keep going, because your mind is shifting into the spiritual realm.

To get help from any spirit, understand that all spirits have a particular influence they operate within. Some say that spirits vibrate on a particular frequency. Therefore, the first step in contacting a spirit is to create a familiar environment for it. A lot of traditions (including religions) recommend burning incense, lighting candles, performing cleansing rituals, fasting, or praying. These are great tools to help you zero in, but the whole purpose of all these techniques is to align your mind and heart.

There are numerous ways to contact spirits, but I consider the simplest method involves any technique that doesn't require any tools—except for your mind. The idea is that even if you do not have access to tools (e.g., herbs, incense, oils, etc.), you should still be able to contact a spirit even while you are driving your car, amongst a crowd of people, or anywhere else. The simplest way I have found to get into a particular state of mind to contact any spirit is by taking on a magickal authority by:

1. Saying the Lord's Prayer: Psalm 23, or any other appropriate prayer to your Higher Power, which is essentially your Higher Self.

2. Calling the name of the spirit: Focus your thoughts and feelings to determine if the spirit has responded.

3. Stating your desire: Clearly express what it is that you want and how fulfilling that desire will make you feel.

4. Make an offering: Or pay the spirit for their assistance. This step is important because we have all been conditioned (both human beings and spirits) to believe that you do not get something for nothing. So,

at the least, say "Thank you." Ideally, pay the spirit something to express your gratitude, such as a candle, flowers, water, liquor, or candy. Ignore the foolish horror movie clichés and put down the dagger, spirits do not want your blood. Spirits want time and energy. The reason material offerings are accepted the most is because they are easier to provide. However, if you prefer to devote your time and energy to a cause, like volunteering at a food pantry or running a marathon in the name of the spirit, that's perfectly fine. The choice is yours, and the agreement is between you and the spirit.

5. Let it go: Go about your business and let the spirit do what you asked. Meaning, stop thinking about it. Distract yourself with something totally unrelated and let the spirit work on your behalf.

These are the basic steps to contacting any spirit. Feel free to adapt or modify them according to your intuition because the spirit you choose may prefer that you contact them in a particular manner. For instance, some spirits might prefer that instead of you praying that you perform a ritual libation followed by incense, while other spirits might favor a prayer combined with spraying alcohol and tobacco smoke. Most Roman Catholic churches use prayers, fan incense, and sprinkle holy water, whereas Protestant churches focus solely on prayer. So, as you can see, there is no right or wrong way, except for what works.

Before concluding this section, there are two things that need to be kept in mind when communicating with spirits, and they are:

1) Spirits are not superior to human beings. They are simply entities that do not have a physical body, so they are not limited to time and space as we are. This allows them to see into the future and influence the thoughts and actions of others. However, spirits cannot make you instantly rich or instantly heal you. They are not a replacement or substitution for your own mind and will. Spirits can provide insights and guidance beyond our normal perception. For instance, if you contact a spirit to help heal your body or recover from an illness, it may see the future consequences of you consuming a particular food and will intuitively guide you away from foods that could worsen your condition.

2) It is important that you do not send spirits mixed messages by focusing on our current condition of what you don't want. Be mindful of focusing on what you want, now what you lack. In our fast-paced, instant-gratification, supersized-society, it is common to focus on what you don't have. If you want more money, for example, don't spend time complaining about being broke. Doing so sends a mixed message to the spiritual realm, signaling that you desire more of the same lack because this is what you are focusing a lot of your time and energy on. Instead, you must focus on what you want. Visualize what you would do with more money or how having it would change your life. If you want more money and prosperity, then you must keep a clear image in mind of why you want more money or what you would do with more money. If you want healing, imagine yourself engaging in activities you would enjoy if you were already well. If you are unhappy in your job,

imagine a better working environment. Holding a clear picture of your desired end result communicates to spirits what you truly want.

Chapter 3: Two Types of Spirits

Through my personal experience and research, I theorize that there are two types of spirits that exist, and I classify these spirits based on how they interact with energy. First, there is only one energy source that exists. You can call this energy source the Universe or God. The Chinese refer to it as Chi, Christians call it the Holy Ghost, while the Kemetic sages called it the Power of God or Ra/Rau, symbolizing it as the Sun.

Now, according to the law of thermodynamics, we know that energy cannot be created or destroyed, but it can be transformed. This understanding has led me to conclude that, since there is only one energy Source or Rau, which is symbolized by the Sun, there must be two types of spirits that exist: those that need energy and those that can manipulate energy.

The spirits that need energy are what I classify as spirits that exist outside of us, while the spirits that manipulate energy are those that exist within us. In essence, all spirits are metaphysical beings, representing different aspects of ourselves that we manifest into existence.

The Spirits Within

Keeping in mind what was mentioned about Consciousness in "Someone Lied: Consciousness is Not Just in the Brain," the spirits that exist within us can be found in the cosmos, in nature, and within our physical being. This is because they are basically natural energies that have been anthropomorphized to help us to get a better understanding of how the universe functions both within and outside of our being. For instance, fire, in most cultures, is understood to be red, hot, masculine, etc., so in most lore, this energy is depicted as a male deity.

Within our being, the spirits that exist in all of us correspond to various clusters and/or psychic centers in our mind, which are commonly referred to as spheres in Tree of Life traditions or chakras in Yogic traditions. These spirits have been called numerous names throughout history, such as spirit of nature, gods, goddesses, angels, demons, etc., but from my research and understanding. Psychologically speaking, these spirits are archetypal energies, which are the unconscious forces that drive and shape us through archetypes. For example, a few of the most common archetypes whose recurring behavior, personality and symbols can be found in folklore across the globe are "The Trickster," "The Mother," and "The Sage." The "Trickster" archetypal energy embodies confusion, disruption, playfulness, mischief, and the ability to challenge societal norms, while often acting as a catalyst for change through unpredictable behavior. The "Mother" exemplifies "concern for safety, protection, compassion, nurturing, love, and fertility." While the archetypal energy of the "Sage" is characterized by a passionate thirst for knowledge, wisdom, and truth that is frequently portrayed as a wise, usually recluse and austere mentor. However, I should warn you that although these are mental constructs, archetypes interact with us (the "I" part of our being) on a daily basis as if they are separate entities, regardless of whether we believe in them or not.

The spirits within us do not need energy or offerings per se, because they have mastered the ability to transform energy for their survival. This explains why these archetypes can be found in various cultures around the world.

How did these spirits come into existence, and where did they come from? I believe that, once upon a time, these spirits were living human beings, and when they died, they were honored as external spirits. Over time, they were eventually deified.

The Spirits Without

Again, keeping in mind what was said about Consciousness, the spirits that are said to exist outside of us simply exist beyond our awareness. These include astrological forces, thought forms, and the spirits of the dead, all of which are so intricately connected to our Awareness that their influences are typically interpreted as normal. However, these are all hidden forces that have the ability to influence human thought.

Generally speaking, astrological forces, or what we call the zodiac, can influence our emotions. But most of the time, we ignore these influences because we are not animals who live purely by our emotional instincts.

Thought forms are essentially thoughts that have been repeated so frequently that they take on a life of their own.

The spirits of the dead are the souls of people who have lived and died, but their eternal soul continues to exist because it is energy, which cannot be created or destroyed.

For the purpose of this book, we will focus on the spirits that have the most influence in our lives: the spirits of the dead. These spirits of the dead are especially influential because they were once human beings, and when they died, they acquired the ability to influence our thoughts, and as such, our actions.

I remember that Papa taught me that the one thing to understand about spirits of the dead is that just because they do not have a physical body does not mean they are wiser or more knowledgeable than us. Since these spirits do not have a physical body, they are not limited as we are and can travel anywhere, at any time, in a fraction of a second. This means that the spirits of the dead know how we think and how to influence us because they were once like us. Their lack of a physical body allows them to see far into the future because they are no longer bound by time and space, unlike those of us who have a physical form. Understanding this simple concept will prevent you from falling into the trap of worshiping spirits, as so many other people have done.

When you keep this in mind and recognize that spirits are just like people, you'll understand that, just as there are good and bad people, there are good and bad spirits also. Just like people may not get along because of personality differences, spirits can have personality conflicts with you. This is why it is always advised to work first and foremost with your ancestors.

There are numerous theories on why and how spirits exist, but this is my best understanding of it. For the record, I must confess that it took me a minute to really understand this theory but once I pictured the Superconscious as a government organization. Then, I thought about how within the government there are numerous departments, like the Department of Finance & Treasury, the Department of the Arts, Department of War, the Executive Department better known as the Executive Branch, etc. It began to make more sense how our Superconscious functions in our life. From a cultural perspective, instead of seeing the Superconscious as a government and instead viewed it as kingdom. Then, substitute for governmental departments spiritual clans, such as spirits of Maat, spirits of Oset, Hru Aakhuti spirits, and so on. I now had a better understanding and a map of my Spirit.

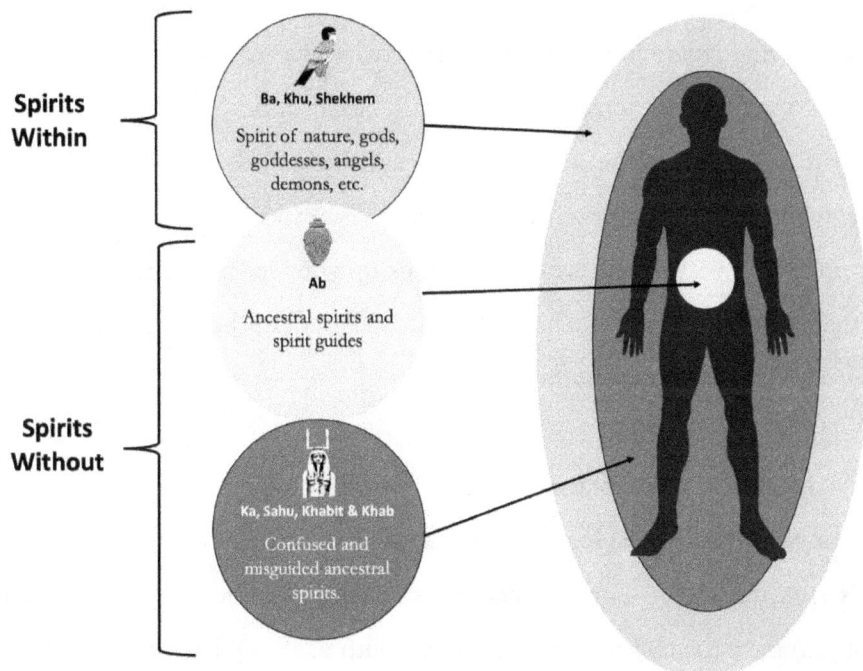

In other words, it can be said that there are spirits that have an influence on you, and spirits you can use to do the influencing. This is very important and should be kept in mind because in future chapters you will see that the ancestor altar is a map symbolizing our entire Consciousness.

In summary, throughout this text, spirits that exist within are referred to as archetypes, forms, gods, goddesses, etc., because this is the best way for most human beings to comprehend these entities from an intellectual perspective. There are numerous ways to communicate and interact with the spirits within. The best way is to consciously work with these energies within you for personal growth and self-awareness is by journaling, meditating, and view them as living beings, similar to your family and friends, hence the reason they are also referred to as "familiar" spirits (note the key word "family").

The spirits that exist without include astrological forces, thought forms, and all of the spirits of the dead. Again, this is based upon perception, but it is easier for us, as human beings, to understand how these entities exist on an intellectual level. Otherwise, you may spend countless hours trying to figure out if spirits are real or not, which will muck up your spiritual practice. Simply put, magic occurs when you have fewer thoughts and become receptive to your BA (Higher Spirit or Superconscious).

What you should understand is that all spirits have the ability to cause synchronistic events. The level or degree of this influence depends upon the spirit's spiritual ability. For instance, most netcharu (which you will meet in Chapter 5) have the ability to communicate with us using the forces of nature, such as animals, plants, the wind, etc. Whereas lower spirits have the ability to influence people in your favor.

Chapter 4: What and Who are Our Ancestors?

Ancestral Memories

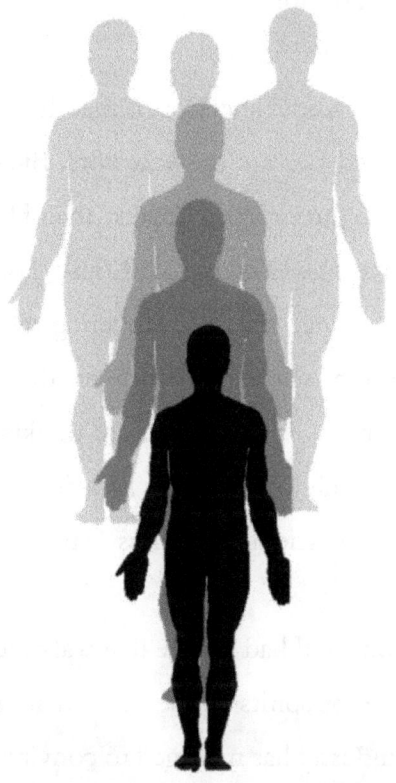

Generally, when one says "ancestors," they are basically referring to a specific group of spirits who were our blood relatives. But you can also have ancestors who were not biologically related to you but still cared for your wellbeing, such as a godparent, foster parent, adoptive parent, etc.

So, your ancestors are your deceased relatives who form an ancestral link back to the first of your lineage to walk the planet. They are also the souls of the deceased who cared for you that may or may not be biologically related to you, which is commonly referred to as spirit guides. Both biological ancestors (biological aakhu) and spirits guides are called aakhu in the Kemetic language, which means "stars" a metaphor for them being guides in the night sky. They all need energy to continue to exist, which can come from anything that has Rau, such as food, water, or drink.

One big misunderstanding about ancestors is that they are separate beings. No, the ancestors are you, and you are the ancestors. Biologically speaking, your ancestors continue to live through you because their blood flows through your veins. Keeping in mind what was said about Consciousness, you are simply the last physical link of your ancestral line. Hovering over you is a long line of ancestors, which Western science belittles to the concept of "ancestral memories." What this means is that if you are thinking about your deceased grandfather, you are basically retrieving or bringing back all of his memories and experiences to your conscious awareness (Ab).

But, just as there are good and bad people that walk the planet, there are good and bad souls of people, or spirits of the dead, that exist in the spirit world. While the horror film industry has managed to convince people to believe that ghostly spirits are evil and demonic, the truth is that most negative spirits were simply negative people in life.

How did these people become negative; you ask? It is the same way people become negative in life: they make fatal and unwise decisions based on their ignorance, confusion, and misguidance. Due to these serious missteps, they lived a miserable existence, leeching off of people. And since death is a reflection of one's life, they continue to exist as miserable spirits called aapepu, the Kemetic term for parasitic snakes and worms.

How Do Our Ancestors Communicate with Us?

Our ancestors communicate with us all the time because they are the closest external forces to us that exist in the universe. The reason most of us do not recognize when our ancestors (or any other spirits, for that matter) are communicating is because we are usually in a beta mind state, which prevents us from having an open mind. If you begin to relax your mind and body, you will eventually enter into an alpha mind state. The more you relax your mind and body, the more your consciousness shifts into a higher state of trance, and the more intuitive you become. One way to encourage intuitive communication with your ancestors is by using your third eye.

The third eye is the area between your eyes on your forehead, which corresponds to your pituitary gland. Contrary to popular belief, the third eye does not give you heightened psychic abilities or superpowers. Mystics called it the third eye because the region between your eyes gives us the ability to visualize clearly and use your extrasensory abilities while in a higher trance state. These extrasensory abilities, commonly called psychic abilities, are:

- Clairvoyance is the ability to perceive things or events in the future without the use of your physical senses. If you are clairvoyant, you might see things floating in the corners of your eye, have vivid dreams, see flashes of light, colors, numbers, or symbols, envision things in your mind's eye, or see images in your mind upon hearing or reading about them. The Spanish word celaje (pronounced say-la-hay) refers to these kinds of visions.
- Clairaudience is the ability to perceive things or events through hearing. If you have this ability, you might hear ringing or buzzing noises in your ears, popping ear pressure, and/or voices. Society has

convinced us that when we hear voices that we are "crazy," but the difference between mental illness and individuals with clairaudient abilities is that the latter can control the voices that are speaking to them, whereas the mentally ill person cannot.

- Clairsentience is the ability to perceive things through your feelings. For instance, you can sense the emotions of animals, plants, and people, as well as detect when spirits are around you.
- Claircognizance is the psychic ability to receive messages intuitively. Most claircognizants simply receive ideas out of the blue that are usually 100% accurate. Out of all the psychic abilities, claircognizance is the most controversial because messages are said to come or be channeled from a spirit. If you are claircognizant, you might come off as a know-it-all, have a knack for sizing people up without them telling you much about them, be good at solving problems, misplace things but visualize where they are in your mind's eye, and know things without people telling you.

One of the simplest ways I have found to awaken your third eye and encourage constructive dialogue with your ancestors is to activate it like you did when you were a child. If you recall, as a child, if you were a boy, you played with race cars, GI Joe figures, or *Star Wars* action figures. Girls often pretended to cook or hosted a tea party with all their doll friends. Basically, if you played make-believe in any way, your third eye was activated. Therefore, by putting yourself back in that imaginative mindset, you can experience some of the psychic abilities described above. If you imagine talking to your ancestors, so long as you do not answer back, you can increase your communication with them.

How to See Your Spirits

Seeing spirits is actually an easy thing to do, it simply requires that you use your imagination. First, close your eyes and imagine the room you are in. Now, imagine seeing a black dog. It does not matter what kind of dog it is, and the picture does not have to be crystal clear. Just imagine seeing a black dog with your eyes closed. Next, visualize the dog having blue eyes.

Once you have done this, open your eyes and imagine the dog sitting in front of you with those blue eyes. Again, the image will not be crystal clear, but you should be able to get a good impression. Remember, you're not seeing the image with your physical eyes, but with your mental or spiritual eyes. This is how all spirits (ancestors, spirit guides, guardian spirits, saints, gods, goddesses) appear to us.

You can also smell, hear, and touch spirits the same way. But understand that it is not through your physical senses, but through your spiritual senses, that you are able to see and interact with them.

3 Reasons Why You Should Venerate Your Ancestors

If you grew up in a Western society, then honoring the ancestors will feel weird because we have all been taught that it is best to leave those who have passed alone. We have been taught to simply let them rest until they can be called back to "Glory" when God returns. But it has been a long-standing belief within the African American community that our ancestors are concerned about our wellbeing. It is also a long-standing belief that our ancestors communicate with us through our dreams, even though this was never explicitly taught in the church. This is the reason a lot of African American churches have photos, pews (church benches), rooms, and other items dedicated to the memory of certain ancestors. The quiet reason behind these dedications to these ancestors is to improve the "good luck" of the church.

Now, if you grew up in the church like I did, then you were probably also taught by overzealous adherents that there is no such thing as good luck. You were likely encouraged to believe only in the power of God, but I found that this isn't always totally effective because:

1) For most of us, God is the most ambiguous and abstract being in existence, so it is hard to fully believe in something that we do not truly comprehend.

2) I also found that good luck and bad luck are largely influenced by our thoughts and behaviors. I discovered this one day after buying my first car and worrying that I would get into an accident because I did not have insurance when I drove it off the lot. Surely enough, I got in an accident the next day, which taught me that I created my own bad luck with my thoughts of worry.

Here are some of the easiest ways to venerate your ancestors and improve your luck:

1. Honor your ancestors by providing them with the nourishment they need to continue to spiritually grow. This is based on the understanding that just as we need physical food to nourish and sustain our physical bodies, our ancestors and spirit guides, who dwell within the spiritual realm, need similar food to nourish and sustain them spiritually. In other words, they need energy.

All spirits receive energy from offerings such as food, water, beverages, money, candles, and flowers. But the purest form of energy they feed on is our attention. The key to attracting and connecting with positive spirits—or getting rid of negative ones—is to either give them attention or ignore them. In other words, to force most negative spirits to leave, all that is usually required is burning something that is offensive to them and, most importantly, ignoring them.

2. The second reason for honoring your ancestors is to prevent them from wandering the spiritual plane as hungry ghosts, begging for attention. Think of attention as a form of currency, when you do not honor your ancestors, you are basically not giving them the "money" they need to take care of their needs. Whenever your ancestors come to mind, you are giving them attention, but a more deliberate way is to set aside time to honor them intentionally.

3. Lastly, honoring your ancestors is crucial because, as I mentioned earlier, they are spirits of the deceased who have the ability to influence your thoughts and behaviors. Since they are spirits without physical bodies, they can also perceive beyond your physical capabilities, seeing far into the past and the future. When you honor them, they are able to provide you with guidance and deter you away from danger. Basically, your ancestors serve as your first line of defense, and they give you good luck.

Honoring your spirits improves your good luck because by doing so, you acknowledge that life continues beyond death and that we are each surrounded by a host of supportive spirits, including with our ancestors. This awareness gives those who venerate their ancestors the courage to proceed in all areas of life, knowing they have invisible support.

A Kemetic Theory on Reincarnation

Now that you understand the importance of honoring your ancestors and spirit guides, it is important to recognize that the foundation of this practice is built upon the belief that our deceased loved ones are still concerned about our wellbeing. The reason our ancestors are concerned is that they want to reincarnate back through us.

Reincarnation is a tricky subject to discuss, mainly because many of us in the West have been taught a non-African theory of reincarnation. According to this popular theory, if you are a bad person, your karma will cause you to be reincarnated back as a dung beetle or some other lowlife form. But if you are a good person, your karma will result in being reincarnated as a wealthy and famous person. From working with my ancestors and spirit guides, I have learned that reincarnation does not occur in this manner. Instead, from my ancestral perspective, reincarnation is about the elevation of consciousness.

To understand this, we must see that everything that exists is a living being, this includes rocks, blades of grass, trees, ants, birds, etc. The difference between human beings and all other beings is that we have a soul, which gives us the ability to make choices and decisions. But how did we get this soul? The soul was born out of a desire, need or want to express and do more. This means human beings are different because we desire or choose to do more. Therefore, all of the life forms that exist on the planet live within a particular cycle. However, once a lifeform desires to do more and becomes conscious, it enters into the human cycle of life, which is an advancement. For instance, once a beetle desires to evolve and become a human being, it cannot revert back into being a beetle. It is like passing kindergarten and being promoted to the next grade level; even if you fail a test, you won't be demoted back to kindergarten. It does not happen because the nature of life is all about advancement and growth.

From this perspective, the reason all humans are not on the same spiritual level or do not have the same level of consciousness is because some human beings have been on the planet numerous times and are "old souls," while others are newcomers or "young souls." I didn't believe in reincarnation until I was shown that throughout my childhood, there were certain things I instinctively would not do because they did not feel right. However, everyone does not have that same psychic sense because it is not a lesson that they have learned in a previous life.

This Kemetic theory of reincarnation explains that the reason some people engage in senseless violence is because typically they are new souls—consciousness that have most likely just left the animal cycle of life and entered the human cycle. Like spoiled children who cannot get their way, they revert to the easiest and most infantile form of communication, which is violence. This is why Set is seen as a symbol of the animal consciousness.

Our ancestors do not want to return and struggle and start all over again in regard to their spiritual development. So, part of the reason they are concerned about our well-being is that, when they choose to reincarnate, they want to have a suitable environment to return to.

3 Rules to Follow to Venerate Your Ancestor Correctly

Now that you understand the importance behind honoring your ancestors and spirit guides, it is time to build an altar. There are numerous ways to do this, and I must state for the record: with so much misinformation circulating on the Internet, there is no single "right" or "wrong" way to honor your ancestors. The truth is, the "wrong way" is what does not work for you and creates future problems, while the "right way" is what works and does not create problems.

It must be remembered, if there were only one way to do things, every culture around the world would be practicing the exact same rituals when it comes to honoring their ancestors, and that is simply not the case. However, after speaking with people from Vietnam, Hong Kong, West Africa, Japan, the Caribbean, and Brazil, about the subject of honoring the ancestors, I have found that there are three basic rules that everyone, regardless of culture, tends to follow:

1. Never, under any circumstances, place a photo of a living person on the ancestor altar. Doing so indicates that the individual is no longer living.
2. Keep your ancestor altar clean and tidy. It should never show any signs of decay.
3. Tend to your ancestor altar regularly. It does not matter how often you tend to the altar. I had friends from Vietnam who tended to their ancestor altar every day, people I knew from the Caribbean who swore that you should only tend to your ancestor altar once a week. Some of these same Caribbean friends also suggested tending to the ancestor altar on Monday, as it is the start of the workweek and is considered the luckiest day of the week.

I mention these examples to illustrate that such practices are influenced by cultural perception and by beliefs. For instance, in North America, Monday is one of the busiest days of the week. Although I understand the logic behind honoring my ancestors on a Monday or Friday, I personally do not think our ancestors care about which day we choose as long as we are consistent. So, the days of the week where I can consistently honor them are on Saturdays and Sundays. The key is to choose a day that is convenient for you.

To help you, I have included a list of what each day symbolizes, and the corresponding energy and celestial body associated with the day.

Day of the Week	Corresponding Netchar	Significance
Hrushomt (Monday)	Oset	Ruled by the Moon. Optimal day for performing rituals for prosperity, appeasement, dreams, receptivity, female fertility and to initiate new business undertakings.
Hrufedu (Tuesday)	Hru Aakhuti	Ruled by the Mars. Optimal day for performing rituals for breaking curses and overcoming enemies and conflict, overcoming business competitors, and creating strife and bitterness among friends.
Hrudu (Wednesday)	Npu	Ruled by the Mercury. Optimal day for performing rituals spiritual development, communication and influencing others because it is considered a day of slip-ups.
Hrusesu (Thursday)	Ma'at	Ruled by the Jupiter. Optimal day for performing rituals for wealth, success in your career, and for beginning long-term projects.
Hrusefk (Friday)	Nebthet	Ruled by the Venus. Optimal day for performing rituals for beauty, love and romance.
Hruwa (Saturday)	Sokar-Ptah	Ruled by the Saturn. Optimal day for performing rituals for psychic self defense, spiritual protection, home protection, and for making protective charms.
Hrusenu (Sunday)	Hru	Ruled by the Sun. Optimal day for performing rituals favor from people of authority, honor, diplomacy, preparing charms for health and longevity, and settling differences.

Frequently Asked Questions About Honoring the Ancestors

Does ancestor veneration depend on blood type?

Contrary to popular belief, ancestor veneration is not dependent on matching blood types. It also does not require that you honor everyone on your family tree or know everyone in your family lineage. The theory is that because spirits do not have a physical body, our ancestors can see our ancestral ties going all the way back to the beginning of time. This is because there is an unbroken chain of blood connecting you to the first human on Earth, so adoptees have no need to worry. If you are adopted and choose to honor your ancestors, they will know who you are even if you do not know them.

Do I have to honor everyone, such as individuals who were abusive and traumatized others?

The answer is no. You are not obligated in any way to honor or venerate anyone. This is your life, and one of the reasons for honoring your ancestors in the first place is to improve the quality of your life by tapping into their wisdom, not them living your life through you. If you do not want to honor a particular ancestor, you do not have to. In fact, if you choose not to honor a group of your ancestors, you can skip them entirely. Historically, this was suitable punishment.

The Kemetic people were known for being the most detailed record-keepers in ancient times because they documented everything in stone. But they are also known for punishing souls by removing the names of individuals from monuments and their documents, especially if those individuals caused major problems. The most famous example of this was the heretic king Akhenaten, whose so-called monotheistic religion nearly led to Kemet being conquered by the Assyrians. Again, you are in charge of your ancestor altar, and the only rules you need to follow are the three rules.

How do I make contact with my ancestors or spirit guides?

Ancestors and spirit guides usually communicate with the living via dreams and by influencing people. So, when these spirits reach out, synchronicities often occur because we are all connected. For instance, if you wanted to connect with Malcolm X, you might start by reading his autobiography, watching movies about him, and immersing yourself in his story. Then, one day, you might have a dream where Malcolm speaks to you, or someone says something that reminds you of him, or you might display some characteristics that Malcolm had. These are all signs that Malcolm is communicating with you.

What if I am of mixed heritage?

Recently, there's been a lot of focus on whether being of mixed heritage affects ancestral connections, often based on skin color. But family, your heritage is not based upon the color of your skin, it's about the culture you identify with the most. The reason you are reading this book is because you identify with African culture the most. So trust your intuition and do not let this matter hinder you. Trust your ancestors, and if you need clarity on this issue, allow them to speak and give you peace of mind.

When can I place an ancestor on my ancestor altar?

Typically, it is advised to place ancestors on the altar who have been dead for longer than a year and have died from natural causes. The belief is that the newly departed need time to get acclimated to their new role as a spirit. You generally do not want to include people who were murdered, died from substance abuse, or had extreme mental illnesses, as those souls are often very troubled and will need additional spiritual assistance beyond what you may be able to provide.

Your ancestor altar is a microcosm of your life, so if you place energies on your altar that conflict with you, you will see that conflict manifest in your life. Essentially, you want to place ancestors on your altar who support you and not add a lot of things, so that communication will be clear.

Can I put anything on the ancestor altar?
Yes and no. While you can put whatever you want on the ancestor altar, remember that it is not for you, it is for your ancestors. The altar is meant to make them feel comfortable so that they can communicate with you at ease. So, if your ancestors were Christian, for example, then you would include a bible or things that they enjoyed.

How long do I leave food offerings on an ancestor altar?
I believe the ancestor altar is a microcosm of your life, so when it comes to making offerings to your ancestors and spirit guides, it is best that you do not allow any offering to decay, rot, or spoil. This is because whatever happens on the altar can manifest itself in your life. Decaying, rotting, or spoiled offerings attract negative energies and negative spirits.

For instance, when my wife and I had our first child, we decided to move closer to my family so that our child could visit with their grandparents. After we moved, it took us a little while to settle in, and for weeks I did not honor my ancestors and spirit guides because I just could not find a suitable place to set the altar. When I finally found a place, I neglected to regularly change the water. At first, I didn't notice, but my wife and I kept getting into little silly arguments, like who left the toilet seat up. These arguments lasted for days. When it finally dawned on me to check my altar, I noticed that the water had become stagnant. Stagnant water is like the water in a marsh or swamp, and it is foul smelling.

Now, I am not saying that because my ancestor altar had stagnant water that it caused my wife and I to argue over foolish things. What I am saying is that my ancestors were blessing our relationship, and when the waters became stagnant, we stopped receiving fresh energy from our ancestors regarding our relationship.

So, never allow anything on your ancestor altar to decay. If you place flowers on your ancestor altar, as soon as the petals start falling remove the flowers. If you place food on the altar, unless it is something like a cookie, bread, or cake, which can probably stay on the altar for up to a week, remove all food offerings the next day. Always refresh your altar at least once a week.

How do I dispose of the food offerings?
Since ancestors are spirits and do not have physical bodies, they cannot consume the food, drink, etc., like we do. Instead, they absorb the essence of the offerings that are given. This means that after you have placed the food on the altar, shortly afterwards, your ancestors will absorb the essence from it.

This is where you must use your intuition. In some cultures, food is offered to the ancestors, allowed to sit for a few minutes, then removed and eaten, as it is believed the ancestors bless the food. In other cultures, the food offerings are discarded at the base of a tree or in the woods, allowing any negative spirits attached to the offerings to leave in peace. Personally, I simply throw the food offerings in the garbage disposal or trash because the essence has already been absorbed. However, you can choose whatever method feels right to you.

What are some offerings that you can give?

- Alcohol – spirits like rum, vodka, beer, wine, and whiskey. It is advised that you do not offer too much alcohol because you do not want your spirits to get drunk.
- Candles – used to enlighten and provide warmth.
- Coffee – black coffee is a good general offering and helps keep your spirits alert.
- Colognes and perfumes – a lot of people have gotten lazy, and simply sprinkle Florida Water, but in the old days, this was the basic fragrance that was used. Spirits actually appreciate and enjoy all fragrances, especially those you wear on a day-to-day basis. If you wear a cologne or perfume, sprinkle or spray some for your spirits to remind them of the pleasantries of life.
- Flowers – flowers remind spirits of the beauty of life.
- Food – a spoonful of your first meal is a meaningful gesture.
- Fruit – represents bounty. While lemons may not be the best choice as they may "sour" things, apples and oranges are greatly appreciated.
- Honey – clover honey is good for money; wildflower honey is used for love and relationships.

- Incense Smoke – transfers messages and intentions to the spirit realm.
- Music – spirits are fond of music, drumming, and songs which may manifest as an "earworm" where a melody stays in your mind.
- Water – the most basic offering that spirits appreciate. Some recommend using spring water only, this is not necessary. It is more important to simply use fresh water that can be obtained easily, such as tap water. If you prefer, you can add energy to the water by praying over it before offering.

What if I don't know who my ancestors are?

When I first started honoring my ancestors, I did not know any of them personally, so I honored cultural heroes who inspired me, like Malcolm X and Martin Luther King Jr. What I found through honoring these historical figures is that they represent the spirit of the culture during their time. Consequently, by honoring these historical figures, it is possible to attract your ancestors to you because they might resonate with the energy of these figures from when they were alive.

What if I didn't like my ancestor when they were alive?

One of the challenges of living in a Western society is that we categorize our experiences as either good or bad based on the pleasure we received from them. However, life is not that simple. There are a lot of things in life that we are not going to like but are ultimately beneficial for us, and the same can be said for ancestors. We must remember that our ancestors were human beings with faults; they were not perfect. They did what they thought was best according to their understanding and their abilities.

That said, this does not give ancestors that were abusive a pass. If you choose not to venerate a particular ancestor, you are not obligated to do so. As mentioned before, this is your ancestor altar, and you can invite whomever you feel will improve your well-being. If you choose not to honor a particular ancestor, simply let them know that they are not welcome and state the reason. You can also tell them that you may choose to honor them at a later date, but for now, they are not welcome. They will understand and respect your decision. If they are truly invested in growth, these ancestors may even try to bring clarity to the issue you have with them.

What do you do if you attract negative spirits?

For the record, anytime you try to do something positive, there is always going to be some negative energy right around the corner. This is one of the truths I had to come to terms with after studying the Story of Osar and learning about Set. That being said, you will occasionally get negative visitors at your altar. When you sense their presence, simply state that your ancestor altar is for honoring your ancestors and spiritual growth, then tell the spirit to peacefully leave and return to where they came from. If the spirit refuses, firmly tell them to leave and burn dragon's blood incense to cleanse the space.

What do you do if you have negative spirits hanging around you?

In my experience, the only danger in honoring your ancestors comes if you inadvertently attract a negative spirit. This typically occurs if you are struggling with issues like physical, sexual, or substance abuse. If you have not fully recovered from these predicaments, you may want to take a coffee bath (see Chapter 6: Practices & Rituals) and burn a little coffee on a charcoal tablet or on the stove. You should also limit your ancestor veneration to simply asking them to help you to fully recover. Pay close attention to your dreams, because you may have an ancestor who overcame a similar issue revealing how they accomplished the feat. I do not mean to preach, but this is why spiritual development is so important, through self-discipline, you can repel certain spirits from your space.

What do you do when ancestors make demands?
Remember, this is your life, and not theirs. As stated earlier, we do not worship our ancestors, which means you are not abiding to their beckoning call. If your ancestors become unruly, you can temporarily discontinue honoring them at any time. Your ancestors who love you and understand the nature of spiritual progress will not be offended by this gesture. Sometimes, you need to do this to detoxify and purge the influences around you.

How do I repel spirits?
If at any time you feel overwhelmed, you can cleanse your space with ammonia and "blessed" (prayed over) salt. Spirits generally dislike ammonia and salt, because it has a crystalline structure, which can trap spirits. You can use these two ingredients separately or together to repel all spirits.

How do I build a basic ancestor altar?
If you already have a painting or photograph of deceased relatives sitting upon a mantle, coffee table, or hanging on a wall, you already have an ancestral altar as a memorial. A memorial is simply a modern version of our Paleolithic ancestors' practice of venerating the dead practice, which often involved keeping the bones. Today, we do not need to keep our ancestors' skulls, but we can keep a photo of them, their ashes, or even dirt from their gravesite.

The idea behind honoring our ancestors is based on the understanding that these are the first spirits we will meet after we die. These spirits are the ones who will most likely have our backs in life. Therefore, the simplest way to honor our ancestors is to elaborate on the memorial by building an ancestor altar.

The ancestor altar can be placed anywhere, such as on the ground, on the floor, on a box, bookshelf, etc. This is a very basic and easy altar that is ideal for people with limited space or those living with others who may not share your spiritual practices.

Start by writing down the names of your deceased relatives and placing the list on the altar. Then, cover it with a white cloth, which symbolizes purity.

Next, place a bowl of tap water and a white candle on the flat surface. You can also include photos of your deceased loved ones on the altar. To make offerings, you might add flowers or other items that you think the spirits would recognize or appreciate. If you include food, do not use salt, as salt repels spirits.

In addition, you can purchase an *Anima Sola(Lonely Soul)* statue or card and place it on the altar to symbolize all the souls that may feel trapped in purgatory, between this world and the next, who are simply floating "out there."

Light the candle and say prayers on behalf of the spirits, like the Lord's Prayer or Psalm 23, and ask God to bless them, give them strength, guidance, and energy. Saying prayers to your spirits will benefit them (even if you don't share their religious beliefs) because it is more meaningful to them than just acknowledging your own beliefs.

This simple practice can quench the thirst of ancestors, soothe lost souls, and "cool" minor poltergeists. To add more potency to your ancestor altar, add items associated with your ancestors, such as dirt from their gravesite. You can also add items they used or would appreciate, like cigarettes, even if you do not smoke—or boiled pork, even if you do not eat it. Remember, these offerings are not for your benefit but for theirs.

As you continue to venerate your ancestors, it is important to pay attention to your dreams. The ancestors are very fond of communicating with us through our dreams, using them to inform you of things they may need in order to help them to help you. If you are new to this practice, it is a good idea to start a dream journal at this time.

Note that the more you venerate your ancestors, the more your ancestor altar will grow. If your ancestor altar expands as you add items that your ancestors were fond of, it might be time to consider building a het, which is a Kemetic shaman altar, described in the next chapter.

Chapter 5: I Lost My Holy Ghost, but Found My Anointing

I must admit, although there are a lot of things I do not like about the church, there were some concepts I was fond of because they are universal and can also be found in the Kemetic spiritual tradition. For instance, the concept known as "the anointing" refers to when spirituality is imbued into an act or practice. When a person does something with "an anointing," it becomes inspiring, uplifting, full of blessings, and spiritual depth because the individual is in direct communication with the Spirit, which is using them as a vessel.

For instance, I really enjoy old-time, bluesy gospel music like *Precious Memories* by Rosette Tharpe because she sings it with an anointing. But I am not a fan of contemporary gospel music because most of it lacks that anointing; it often sounds like they just put some tracks together to make a quick buck. Then, when you hear about all of the drama that these contemporary artists have, it becomes clear how their music is just a reflection of their lives. It's not inspiring at all because they are not living what they preach.

When you live what you know and do things with "the anointing," you're not trying to impress others. Instead, you are doing for others what you would do for yourself. In our merchandising society, where everything costs money, it is difficult to find your anointing, but not impossible. I found my anointing after becoming ill years ago.

As I mentioned at the beginning of this book, Papa was the man who introduced me to Spiritism or Espiritismo. He told me that in Cuba, Espiritismo was how a lot of people venerated their ancestors and honored their spirit guides. He told me that there are numerous spirit guides, and for most people in Cuba, these spirits are in some way associated with one of the African tribes that were brought to Cuba, commonly known as the Seven African Powers. To explain his point, he pointed to a stereotypical "mammy" statue he had standing alongside the wall, which he called La Madama. The statue was adorned with a scarf and hat. Papa told me that his La Madama was his Ellegua's wife, a female spirit who was most likely crowned with Ellegua when she was alive and now honored as a spirit guide.

Papa went on to describe the spiritual hierarchy, which starts with Papa Dios – Father God or the Supreme Being, also called the Man Upstairs. Below Papa Dios are the orishas, saints, and other deities, such as the Taino and Arawak divinities. Under them are the spirit guides, followed by the ancestors.

Papa told me that the goal in Espiritismo is spiritual enlightenment and evolution for yourself and others (including spirits). Typically, spiritual work is done by honoring these spirits on an altar called a bóveda espiritual, or simply a bóveda. This involves offering the spirits Catholic prayers and/or prayers from Allan Kardec's book *Collection of Selected Prayers*, heeding their guidance, and offering them spiritual energy through light, unsalted food, drinks, and other things that they may have enjoyed in life. In this way, the energy offered to the spirits of the dead is returned to us (the living) in the form of spiritual assistance, spiritual guidance, spiritual protection and spiritual support, allowing the spirits to work through us to help us accomplish our physical goals through good luck.

Before I became ill, I initially tried to mimic Papa's bóveda. In the olden days, due to the very brief Spiritualism Movement that spread throughout the United States, followed by the Holiness and eventually the Pentecostal Movement, most folks did not specifically classify spirits. Many felt that it was too secular. Since Spiritism was not Bible based, a lot of Christians believed that further exploration into the subject matter would lead one away from Jesus and down a demonic path. As a result, many people, especially those in the Pentecostal churches, simply referred to spirits in broad terms: spirits of God, demonic spirits, devilish spirits, spirit of envy, illness or cancerous spirits, spirits of poverty, sweet spirits, hot spirits, and so on. Papa's explanation about spirits and his spiritual hierarchy made sense to me, even though it was initially unfamiliar.

In fact, I remember as a kid growing up, my younger brother and I would always get into arguments on Sunday afternoons after church. So, my mom would "fix" us by going back to church for the Sunday night church service, making my brother and I sit on the front pew to drive the devil out of us. Every now and then, my brother and I would get smart and be the most loving siblings ever, at least until 7:00 p.m., hoping it would be too late to make it to evening service. But my mother was not always impressed; she would take us to church anyway. (Laughs)

But as I mentioned, when I got older and begged for the Holy Ghost to descend upon me so that I could be saved from the drug-related violence occurring in the streets of Detroit, I lost my Holy Ghost several weeks later. This led me to closely observe the actions and behaviors of those around me who still had their Holy Ghost. I noticed that as soon as the music and drums began playing, the Holy Ghost would descend. Some people seemed able to get the Holy Ghost at will, while others would fake it. The most alarming thing I noticed was that some people who got the Holy Ghost could be ornery and bitter individuals, but once the Holy Ghost fell upon them, it resulted in them dancing and speaking in tongues. Yet, moments later, the Holy Ghost would leave, and the individual would revert back to their ornery ways.

Later, when I decided to leave the church and began reading books in an attempt to learn more about the Kemetic religion and traditional African religions in general, one of the first books I read was Luisah Teish's *Jambalaya: The Natural Woman's Book of Personal Charms and Practical Rituals* and in it, she states:

> "'Getting the spirit' in the Holiness and Baptist churches of the U.S. South is similar to possession in rituals of Haiti and Nigeria. It involves altered states of consciousness and manifests through shaking and 'talking in tongues.' The utterances made through 'talking in tongues' are heavily voweled, much like the languages of West Africa."

Teish also states:

"In Black Christianity, the force possessing the person is usually identified as Jesus Christ or the Holy Spirit. In the religions more clearly aligned with African beliefs, the force is identified as a specific ancestor or deity. Furthermore, the possessed Baptism most often delivers testimony on the power and goodness of the spirit, whereas in egun (ancestor) and orisha (deity) possession, information directly relevant to the welfare of the human community is given."

After I became ill, I started working with my ancestors and spirit guides more intimately based upon my cultural perspective because: 1) my basic ancestor altar, described in Chapter 4 of this book, had outgrown itself, and 2) years ago, Papa had encouraged me to study my own ancestral traditions. So, I decided to move beyond Papa's interpretation of the spiritual hierarchy.

When I did, to my surprise, I found that Spiritism/Espiritismo was actually founded by a 19th-century French educator, translator, and writer named Hippolyte Léon Denizard Rivail (3 October 1804 – 31 March 1869), who wrote under the pen name Allan Kardec. Through investigating psychic mediums, Kardec defined the belief that the soul continues to exist after death and that it is possible to talk to them. Kardec explained that not all spirits had the same level of maturity and stated in The Spirits Book that spirits are organized into a rigid spiritual hierarchy, arranged into three orders and ten classes:

I. **The First Order or Pure Spirits** is the highest order of spirits. Through a series of reincarnations, these spirits no longer have to reincarnate because they have obtained a superior level of intelligence and morality.
   1. Pure Spirits
   2. High Spirits
   3. Wise Spirits

II. **The Second Order or Good Spirits** consists of spirits who prioritize spirit over matter. Generally, these spirits are good and want to ascend to a higher level, but they still have imperfections they need to address. Good spirits are divided into four classes:

4. Learned Spirits
5. Caring Spirits
6. Boisterous Spirits
7. Neutral Spirits

III. **The Third Order or Imperfect Spirits** are solely focused on and influenced by their material desires. They are ignorant, selfish, and full of false pride.

8. Lying Spirits
9. Frivolous Spirits
10. Impure Spirits

When I thought about Kardec's spiritual hierarchy and took into consideration what Teish said about Black Christianity, the Holy Ghost, and spirit possession in African religions, and then compared this to what I learned about Spiritism based upon my experience with the Holy Ghost and the detrimental state that my community was in, I concluded. It was not the Holy Ghost that had descended upon me, but rather a low-level ancestral spirit. This meant to me that the reason my life (and many other peoples' lives, including the community) did not significantly change after we received the Holy Ghost was that we had a low-level spirit impersonating a wiser one. These were the spirits that some refer to as trickster spirits.

That was when the light came on, and I realized that the reason African Americans' lives were not significantly changing was because we had been dealing with low level ancestral spirits (Third Order in Kardec's spiritual hierarchy) that could not offer any wisdom to improve our lives.

Why is Kemet (Ancient Egypt) So Important?

When I asked my Spirits why they encouraged me to learn about the Kemetic religion, they told me that it was because the Kemetic religion, by the way of the Story of Osar, was the only way that I would start honoring my ancestors.

They told me that through honoring my ancestors, I would have come to know God, similar to how Hru venerated his ancestor Osar and awakened his own divinity. (Osar symbolizes Hru's ancestors and is also the personification of the Superconscious).

That's when it also became apparent why so much effort is made to conceal the fact that the Kemetic people were black and brown-skinned Africans. For example, there is the selective cherry-picking and performing in DNA testing on Nefertiti, the boy king Tutankhamen's mother, while avoiding the same DNA test on Tutankhamen's grandmother, Queen Tiye (shown on the left). This is because, if people knew that the Kemetic people were black and brown Africans, they would learn that the Kemetic religion was based upon the understanding that God is within. This realization would encourage people to study the Kemetic religion, eventually discovering that the Kemetic people, like other traditional Africans,

practiced spirit possession. It was through spirit possession, particularly invoking the ancestors, that Kemet became such a highly advanced society.

Imagine, instead of reinventing the wheel, you could simply pick up where your ancestor or a spirit guide left off. Imagine tapping into someone else's experience to learn a particular technique that would benefit your family.

All of this knowledge led me to convert my bóveda into a het aakhu (ancestor and spirit guide house), which not only honored my aakhu but also helped me program my mind (Superconscious/subconscious) to create the life that I wanted.

The Kamta Way

This new perspective made me see the Story of Osar as an allegorical tale about tribal clans who fought to unify the kingdom, a story that ancient Kemetic shamans also used to unify the human mind.

In Genesis 1:26, it is said that we are made in the image of God, but most theologians gloss over this scripture because they do not understand who and what God really is. It is more convenient for non-initiates to say that God is omnipotent, omniscient and omnipresent, thus keeping the Creator incomprehensible, inconceivable, and unimaginable-a reference point for when things don't work out. Hence, the reason people call upon God when all else fails is because of religious indoctrination.

But God is All, and All is God, which means God is Everything. We are all a part of God, and God is all a part of us. For simplicity's purpose, it is easier to say that God or the Divine is the Universe, and we are a microcosm of that

Macrocosm. This means that all of the attributes and qualities of the Divine exist within our being, but on a smaller and minute scale, similar to how a droplet of water retains the same qualities (though not the quantity) of the ocean. We are all fragments of the Divine's Mind because the Universe is Mental, and the Mind is All, which is the Divine.

Since the Divine is eternal, by deductive reasoning the part of us that is made in the image of the Divine is not our body but our mind. In other words, there is a Superconscious part of the Divine, a subconscious part, and a conscious part, the latter being you.

Remember, the Superconscious and subconscious are not the same. The main difference between the two is that every time you learn something new, it is your subconscious that feels fear or resistance to change, preferring to stick to old habits. The Kemetic sages understood this, which is why they symbolized the Superconscious as Osar (Asar, Ausar, Osiris), Hru as the conscious, and the subconscious as Set (Set-an).

This means that the eternal battle between the so-called forces of good and evil, allegorized in the Kemetic legend as Osar versus Set, is really a battle between our Superconscious (Higher Self) and subconscious (lower self).

Therefore, all of the so-called deities, gods, and goddesses of mythological lore are actually energies that exist throughout the universe and within our mind that have been personified. In other words, all of the gods, goddesses, demons, and spirits are simply different components of our Superconscious, conscious, and subconscious minds. Whereas the Superconscious relates to the unknown parts of the Universe, and the subconscious to the known parts of the Universe, while your conscious mind is the decision-maker.

Instead of three Kardecian orders, I saw these types of spirits or energies as existing both around us and within us. These energies Kardec referred to as classes are, in the Kongo tradition, the BaSimbi (benevolent spirits), BaKulu (ancestral spirits), and BaNkyu (malevolent spirits). In Kemet, they were known as the Netcharu (guardian spirits), Aakhu (ancestors and spirit guides), and Aapepu (confused and misguided, malevolent ancestral spirits).

This means that instead of honoring and venerating only a few ancestors that you know of you now are able to honor and venerate your entire tribal clan spirits, other tribal clan spirits, as well as any spirit that is associated with a particular energy or netchar. In other words, each netchar has a number of spirits surrounding and supporting it. For instance, Npu is the divine energy that finds lost things, grants good luck, opens pathways, and offers personal protection and guidance. However, since it is impossible for him to be in more than one place at a time, he has spirits assigned to him that will assist him in his task. These aakhu may or may not be deceased blood relatives, but they act as guides on Npu's behalf.

Therefore, the ancestor altar from this perspective becomes a spiritual programming tool and a gateway that will help you to explore the mysteries of the Spirit and use it to improve your life.

The Netcharu: Guardian & Totem Spirits

The netcharu (or netchars) are archetypal energies and spirits of Netchar (Nature) that symbolize particular Kemetic tribes, clans, families, or individuals. Initially, these netcharu, or nature spirits, were viewed as familial guardians, offering spiritual protection to tribes. These spirits were believed to control natural phenomena, such as rises in tides or strong winds, and they were called upon for help with crops, successful hunts, protection from rival tribes, etc.

Clan heads and chiefs relied upon these spirits for their wisdom, because the netcharu were seen as deified ancestors whose biological lineage had been lost, similar to the origins of other mystical and angelic beings.

Initially, there were ten netcharu, but due to Set's actions and behaviors, he was excluded to symbolize the nine forces of nature or nine clans who fought to unify Kemet.

The nine netcharu are recognized as the main guardians of Kemet, but they cannot work together at the same time. Thus, each person is assigned a totem from the nine netcharu, who walks with him or her for life, both in the physical and spiritual realms. This totem spirit acts as an emissary of the netcharu, but it is not the netchar itself. The totem serves as the individual's main guardian spirit and teacher, having chosen to walk with them. For instance, an individual may have a strong Hru-like personality, but they do not possess the full essence of Hru. Instead, it means their totem radiates strong Hru energy.

This totem creates a connection through shared characteristics, dreams, and interests in animals, linking them back to the netchar. The totem spirit also connects one to the other eight netcharu, and actually orchestrates their efforts in your favor.

The netcharu communicates with us through the totems or spiritual assistants, who give us flashes of insight inspired by objects found in nature, such as rocks, rivers, streams, plants, animals, etc. For instance, to see a hawk, either in real life or in a dream, is a sign that the netchar Hru is speaking to you. Below is a partial listing of the netcharu and the spirits who walk with them:

Osar – is the personification of our Higher Self and symbolizes our Superconscious. He is regarded as the king of the netcharu. The spirits of Osar are calm, ethical, peaceful, and pure. They are fond of the color white and white objects including foods such as rice, ñame, yuca (cassava), and tapioca. Never offer spirits of Osar alcoholic beverages.

Djahuti - embodies the intuitive nature of our Higher Self. He is symbolized

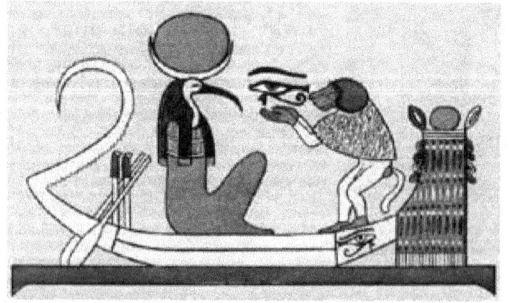

as a man with the mask of an ibis' head. Djahuti was a wise vizier to Osar and served as the interpreter of fate. When Hru fled to him to escape Set, Djahuti's wisdom helped Hru overcome his evil uncle.

Although ever-present, Djahuti makes himself apparent whenever we are having difficulty solving problems, as seen in *the Story of Osar*, where he performs the opening of the mouth ceremony, allowing Osar to speak from beyond the grave. Djahuti is also a shrewd judge who is concerned with settling lawsuits that will bring peace to all involved. He is syncretized with the biblical King Solomon, who was known to be a wise judge and a reputed occultist. The spirits of Djahuti are comprised of spirits that can assist in reconciling any situation peacefully.

Sokar -Ptah – is the name of the energy that governed the cemetery in Kemet, called Sokarra. Thus, Sokar is the representation of the omnipotent nature of our Higher Self and its ability to revive itself. It is symbolized as a mummified man wearing a hawk mask, symbolizing restricted movement and deep contemplation. Sokar manifests itself physically as our skeletal system and embodies the power of healing, persistence, austerity, resistance, and long-suffering. Sokar helps human beings persevere when all of the odds are stacked against them. For this reason, he is considered the patron of cancer survivors, those with a debilitating illness, the

homeless, and all those who have been down on their luck for a long time and are preparing for a comeback. Sokar's spirits assist with healing, spiritual communication, spiritual development, sweeping away negative energies, and performing good and bad magick. Sokar's are fond of the colors black, indigo, brown, and white. The number 13 is sacred to them, as well as working with other Saturnian energies.

Maat – is the personification of our digestive, metabolic, immune, cell production, and maintenance of nutrient systems– all functions performed by our liver. She is envisioned as a mature lady wearing a single ostrich feather on top of her head. Maat is the spirit that helps us maintain balance and live righteously by bringing order and structure into our lives. Some see Maat as the wife of Djahuti, protected by Hru Aakhuti, while others, like me, view Maat as a wise warrior who walks alongside Hru Aakhuti ensuring that his wrath is just. Maat dictates the laws that human beings must follow based upon universal principles. Maat's spirits help one to acquire order, balance, illumination, wisdom, truth, spiritual communication, spiritual abilities, and knowledge. Maats colors are light blue, yellow, and white. Her sacred number is 2. She works harmoniously with numerous nature spirits.

Hru Aakhuti – is the personification of our immune system, as well as hard physical work and physical labor. He is envisioned as a man wearing a hawk-headed mask with feathers designed to incite fright and terror. He is also associated with the winged solar disc which is one of the iconic Kemetic symbols displayed above most entrances.

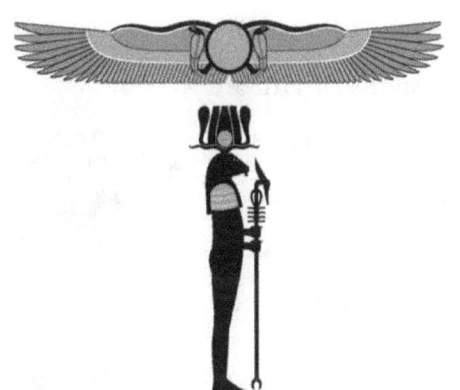

As such, Hru Aakhuti is the netchar who clears paths of all obstacles after Npu discovers the opportunities. For this reason, Hru Aakhuti is considered the owner of all tools and weapons, particularly those made of metal. His spirits

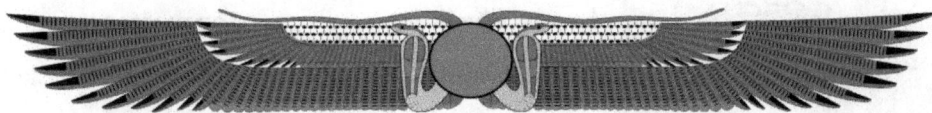

assist with matters regarding justice, enemies, and war. Hru Aakhutis is fond of the colors red, purple, green, and black. His sacred number is 11, and he is aligned with all Martian energies.

Hru – represents the personification of our soul and embodies bravery, courage, masculine beauty, masculinity, fatherhood, royalty, pride, and justice. Hru is imagined as a young male wearing a hawk-headed mask and the double Pschent crown of Kemet. Hru is the spirit that manifests when we have had enough of being walked over or swallowed our pride for the benefit of others.

The difference between Hru and Hru Aakhuti is that Hru Aakhuti is the patron of martyrs, while spirits of Hru are the patrons of heroes and heroines. Spirits of Hru can assist in resolving difficult cases, cleansing stubborn energies, protection, getting revenge or justice, breaking and reversing curses, finding a job, improving one's business, and success in a competition. Hru is associated with the colors red, red and white, and gold. His sacred number is 6.

Nebthet – is the personification of our sexual and reproductive organs, sensuality, love, romance, pleasure, and feminine beauty. She is depicted as a young woman wearing a headdress in the shape of a house with a basket on top. Since sensuality often leads to pregnancy, Nebthet is allegorized as the younger sister of Oset. Nebthet is responsible for attracting people together based upon physical appearances.

Her spirits, like muses, govern art, music, dance, entertainment, as well as things that glitter, like jewelry. Nebthet's sacred colors are yellow, yellow/green, light red, and pink. Her sacred number is 5, and she aligns well with Venusian energies.

Npu – personifies the nervous system and all of the pathways, doorways, roads, and crossroads that lead to opportunities and luck. Npu is imagined as being a young male wearing a wolf- or jackal-headed mask, to represent his protective nature and canine ability to find things, either deliberately or unintentionally. It is this inquisitive nature that links him with curious-minded children, making him playful and lighthearted.

Npu is considered the divine messenger between Osar and humanity. His spirits oversee the opening and closing of one's doorways, finding work or lost objects, bringing prosperity and blessings, and getting luck. Typically, Npu is honored first in rituals to ensure that one does not wander off course. The colors of Npu are red/black, red/black/white, and orange. His sacred numbers are 3, multiples of 3, and 21.

Oset – personifies the reproductive system, as well as family, fertility, femininity, and motherhood. As the protector of families, Kemetic sailors and merchants eventually associated her with the sea and their longing to return back home. Oset is imagined as a beautiful mother wearing a headdress in the shape of a throne, to symbolize her role in nurturing a king.

Her spirits are responsible for helping people change by teaching them about devotion and true love. Oset's sacred numbers are 7 and 21, and her colors are blue, sea blue, and turquoise blue.

I regret that further detailed information could not be given about the netchar here, as it would truly take us beyond the scope of this book. For more information on the netcharu, see the *Maa Aankh* series, *Kamta*, or *The Kamta Primer*.

The Spirits Surrounding Us

Aakhu: Ancestral Spirits and Spirit Guides

The aakhu are ancestral spirits that are closely associated with our conscious mind and spiritual heart. The aakhu typically speak to us through our dreams or our mind's psychic senses. For instance, you may smell a familiar cologne, see an image, hear a sound like a drum, that may make you think of a particular ancestor or spirit guide.

Since I've already discussed ancestors in the previous chapters, to maintain the scope of this book, I will focus briefly here on information regarding the spirit guides.

As mentioned previously, our biological ancestors are called biological aakhu because they are related to us by blood. However, there are other types of aakhu that are also honored and play significant roles in our lives.

Historical Aakhu

Historical aakhu are deceased heroes and heroines after whom buildings, days, and streets are often named. They are usually the ancestors that are remembered for their contributions and associated with a particular era in history. Examples include Fredrick Douglass, Harriet Tubman, Malcolm X, Martin L. King, Jr. etc.

For instance, Malcolm X is an aakhu that anyone can connect with. All you have to do is read his autobiography, study his speeches, or watch movies about him. Engaging with his life and legacy helps establish a connection because he lives on in all of our collective psyche.

What's important to understand is that all spirits, even the aakhu, will communicate with you based upon your level of understanding and experience. In other words, we can all communicate with Malcolm, but he might give me a different message than he gives you because we each have unique perspectives and experiences.

For example, one of the things that Malcolm told me when I was struggling with religious faith, was that the Creator does not care if you call on God, Allah, Yahweh, or any other name. He told me that both he and Dr. King were called to do a job, and there was no way he could have fulfilled his destiny as a Christian. Instead, his path required him to follow the Islamic route. But for other young men, Malcolm has told them that they should follow a route like his as a way to know themselves, starting with joining the Nation of Islam. So, it is all about your perspective and the specific guidance you need.

Cultural Aakhu

Cultural aakhu are ancestors that are similar to historical aakhu but pertain more to cultural practices. Whenever we reinitiate a practice without having any clue as to its African origins, it is believed to have derived from a deep-seated ancestral memory and is being given a new twist.

For example, many of the dances performed by today's youth are prime examples influenced by cultural aakhu. In fact, African American Spirituals (or Negro Spirituals) provide another example. These songs reflected the African population in the American colonies' new faith, sorrows, and hopes during slavery often equating their struggles with the struggles of Jesus and other biblical characters. Spirituals also served as coded messages to help escapees avoid capture. These songs were created by wise men and women who were able to conceal African beliefs.

No one knows the names of the individuals who originated this genre of music, but they are believed to have been among the first Africans to arrive on the shores of North America.

Typically, African American cultural aakhu are imagined as archetypes, such as an old African man called either Papa (Father) or Uncle, and an African woman called Momma (Mother) or Auntie.

The Spirit of Momma or Auntie (La Madama) & the Spirit of Papa or Uncle

Within the African American community, there are a few cultural aakhu that have made themselves known throughout the Afro-Diaspora. In fact, it is possible that, after a few hundred years, some of these aakhu might transcend and become netcharu. These cultural aakhu include the Spirit of Momma or Auntie/La Madama, the Spirit of Papa or Uncle, and Black Hawk. In addition, I am also including information about another Native American aakhu called Sweet Water. Before I explain who, these spirits are, we must understand the importance of cultural aakhu.

Now, the thing that most people do not understand is T.F.A.R.: Thoughts = Feelings = Actions = Results. This means that whatever we think about will create a feeling, which will produce an action and yields a particular result.

Thoughts are communicated and transmitted using images and symbols. Since our subconscious does not know how to reason or distinguish between right and wrong, good or bad, etc., when an image is transmitted, broadcasted, or publicized, if it is not put in context, it is simply accepted as a truth. That being said…

The Spirit of Momma or Auntie/La Madama

One of the most discussed spirit guides nowadays is the famed La Madama, who is honored in both African American and Latin American traditions. La Madama represents a host of female African spirits. In the African American tradition, the La Madamas are believed to be the spirits of old age Black women who practiced conjure and performed divination. In the Latin-American communities, the La Madamas are the spirits of old age Black women who practiced Santeria and/or Palo Mayombe. In both traditions, La Madama is said to represent a wise woman, who is often portrayed as having dark skin, wearing an apron and a headwrap, which is commonly known as a "Mammy" figure.

Historically, it is believed that the Mammies were house slaves who were responsible for caring for the well-being of the slave master and his family. However, American historians who have researched the dynamics of the slave culture have indicated that the "house servant" image is a myth. Although there are historical records that have been recovered, which indicate that there were female slaves that acted as the plantation owner's "right hand," this was very rare because it was not economically feasible for most slave owners.

Patricia Turner, a Professor of African American and African Studies and author of *Ceramic Uncles & Celluloid Mammies: Black Images and Their Influence on Culture*, states that before the Civil War, only the very wealthy whites could afford to use Black women as house servants rather than field hands (p. 44). Turner also claims that usually the house servants were of mixed ethnicity. In fact, historical evidence indicates that the Mammy caricature was created in North America by Southern slave owners to justify and maintain slavery. The Mammy caricature became the most popular image because it ridiculed African American culture, demonized dark skin, depicted Black women as ugly, and portrayed Black people as infantile persons who were happy to serve the slave masters.

This negative portrayal of Black women was broadcasted all over the world and used to sell everything from cookie jars, fishing lures, and ashtrays to laundry detergent, pancake mix, and toys.

In contrast, the Mammy and other African images of women were used to honor and celebrate African culture in the Caribbean and Latin-America. However, these images were used as propaganda tools in North America to promote slavery and degrade Black women. So, if a person from China saw a depiction of a Black woman as a Mammy, they might assume all black women love being domestic servants with no other aspirations beyond happily serving their masters. This stereotype became a programming tool used to create T.F.A.R (Thoughts = Feelings = Actions = Results) to influence how other people think outside of our culture. So, the reason people outside of our community do not respect our women is because they only see one facet of the black woman that has been made into a stereotype.

Therefore, when African Americans started using the term "La Madama" a few decades ago, it was clearly out of respect and a deliberate attempt to restore a fragment of African American heritage and spirituality that had been lost due to the misrepresentation created by a racist society. In most African American communities, the La Madamas were called Mother, Momma, or Auntie out of respect and this custom is still followed to this day.

The first time I encountered a La Madama was through Papa, who said that his La Madama was his Ellegua's wife (meaning she was a spirit guide for his Ellegua). This helped me understand that part of the reason I am so interested in spiritual traditions, divination, etc. likely stems from an African woman ancestor who was interested in these same subjects. As a guide, she may prefer to be called Momma So-and-So or Auntie So-and-So. For instance, in *The Spiritual Churches of New Orleans: Origins, Beliefs, And Rituals of an African-American Religion* by Claude F. Jacobs and Andrew J. Kaslow, a La Madama is known as Aunt Peggy.

My own Auntie spirit assists me in removing foreign influences that conflict with my spiritual development and oppose my cultural beliefs. Therefore, I honor La Madama as Momma or Auntie and petition her to keep peace and security within my home.

The Spirit of Papa or Uncle

In the African American community, typically elderly men of no blood relation are called either "Papa" (Father) or "Uncle" out of respect. This cultural practice stems from the belief in the first Papa or Uncle, who is considered the first African man brought to America as a slave within one's ancestral line. Contrary to popular belief, these men were not passive or accepting of their fate. They were kidnapped, abused, and forcibly shipped to North America, but they did not simply accept their lot in life to slavery or the idea that they were "born in sin." They were deviant, resilient, and rebellious. Whenever an opportunity presented itself for them to rebel against the slave master, they took full advantage of it. Consequently, they used everything within their power to defeat the slave owner. When time aged them, they retained the secrets of their culture and traditions. They passed these on to younger generations, to inspire them to fight for freedom and maintain their dignity.

Therefore, to counter and undermine the influence of the African men, racist southern whites created the Uncle Tom stereotype. For the record, Harriet Beecher Stowe wrote *Uncle Tom's Cabin* to inspire whites to empathize with the slaves and expose slavery as an immoral system. But the Uncle Tom image was twisted and weaponized, portraying Black men as docile, submissive, and content with slavery and proud to be servants. Again, a person not familiar with African American culture would be led to this harmful stereotype that

falsely suggested that all elderly African American men were content with being domestic servants, and thus subjected to disrespect.

The true spirit of African and early African American men during slavery can be found in figures like Josiah Henson (June 15, 1789 – May 5, 1883). Henson, often thought to be the inspiration for *Uncle Tom's Cabin*, was a slave born in Maryland who would later escape to Ontario, Canada. There, he would build a settlement and trade school for other fugitive slaves.

The Papa and Uncle spirit called Preto Velho Pai Bento (Father Bento) or Pai João (Father João) in Brazilian traditions was known as a Kind Uncle according to my research, who typically resided in a bucket of sand adorned with three American flags (symbolizing the trinity). In *The Spiritual Churches of New Orleans: Origins, Beliefs, And Rituals of an African American Religion* by Claude F. Jacobs and Andrew J. Kaslow, it is theorized that Kind Uncle might have been a

Confederate soldier, a spirit linked to the Catholic Saint George, or according to one informant, a deceased relative who died in battle.

To me, this is further proof that the Uncle is an aakhu. Given his rebellious and warrior nature, I believe that the word "Uncle" is a corruption of the Ki-Kongo term Nkisi, thus linking this aakhu to the Kongo spirit.

Thus, Papa and Uncle spirits represent a lineage of elder African and African American male spirits who practiced rootwork and created good luck and protective charms. Many of these spirits were all good and upright men of strong character. They are very bold, blunt, and straightforward. Often suspicious of all people, they were runaway slaves like Josiah Henson, men who refused to have their fate defined by others. Because of their history and principles, they have a strong sense of respect and will only help those who show them proper reverence.

Papa and Uncle spirits are sought after for their wisdom and strength. They know how cruel the world can be and emphasize how important it is to have a strong faith and sharp wits about yourself. They are petitioned to protect the household, to lift curses, and create personal charms for protection and good luck.

Native American Aakhu

Native American aakhu are a distinctive group of spirits who are of Native American ancestry. In recent years there has been a lot of controversy surrounding the idea of African Americans having Native American ancestry. Most DNA testing have revealed that a lot of African Americans who believed they had Native American ancestry do not. However, this test is not completely accurate. The DNA test, to my understanding, indicates the DNA strands that constitute you as an individual. It does not account for all of the DNA strands that contributed to your existence. For instance, National Geographic reported in April 2018, the Race Issue,2 the story of two fraternal twin sisters (Marcia and Millie Biggs) born to a biracial couple, where one twin was distinctly black, and the other twin sister was white. Basically, the Biggs sisters show that the concept of race is not real. Our visible physical characteristics are simply adaptations made by our bodies so that we can survive in the environments we live in.

That being said, Native American aakhu are not honored because they may or may not be blood relatives, but because, during slavery, there were a lot of Native Americans who helped free slaves and helped escapees find freedom. For the record, not all of the Native Americans helped, in fact, some Native Americans owned some African American slaves, just as some African Americans who also owned some slaves, since that was the commerce of the time. However, this was a rare occurrence. Native Americans and African Americans share a unique history, because they were the two largest minority groups in North America. This connection is reflected in our food, language, and cultural practices. Early African Americans borrowed and learned from the Native Americans to help maintain their cultural ways. The distinct difference was that Native Americans literally did whatever they wanted, so quite naturally this led to enslaved early African Americans envying their boldness, courage, and freedom to live and do without restriction.

---

[2] https://www.nationalgeographic.com/magazine/2018/04/race-twins-black-white-biggs/

Native American aakhu all sought the same thing: to maintain and preserve their complete autonomy from the United States. They respected early African Americans who wanted freedom and, to the extent they could, helped those who also sought autonomy as well. Consequently, the Native American aakhu that I have come in contact with through my travels are either the result of intermarriage between Native Americans and African Americans, or respected partners formed through the interaction of the two cultures in the Pequot, Wampanoag, Narragansett, Shinnecock, Creek, Choctaw, and Cherokee tribal nations.

An interesting pattern I have noticed is that many Native American spirits walk closely with either the netchart Maat or Hru Aakhuti. Here are a couple of Native American spirits you might encounter.

Black Hawk and Other Native American Spirits

Usually spirit guides want you to learn something about them, which often reveals something about yourself. For instance, I remember once seeing a Native American statue at a store, so I bought it on a whim. I didn't know why I bought it; I just liked it. I took the statue home, cleaned it, and cleansed it,

then I placed it on an altar. But it didn't feel right, so I moved it. I placed it near another altar, and it still didn't feel right. After some time, I learned that this statue represented Black Hawk, the Sauk leader who went to war against the United States. However, most of what I read about the real Black Hawk did not vibe with me. For instance, my Black Hawk did not want to be placed inside a tin bucket.

To make the long story short, I went through this process for some time until one day I read that some Native Americans would help some early African Americans running from slavery by deliberately misdirecting bounty hunters and others attempting to capture the runaways. It was at that moment that I realized, though not all African Americans may not have had this experience, but since I believe that there is no  such thing as coincidence, this was confirmation to me that this was part of my ancestral past. I placed the statue on my ancestral altar, where it continues to act as a protector.

I have seen many depictions of Black Hawk portrayed as a sitting chief. Personally, I do not recommend purchasing a statue of a sitting Native American chief with a peace pipe unless you plan on giving him his weapons, like stone arrowheads, a knife, toy rifles, etc. I want any matters brought before him to end peacefully, but if he has to knock some heads to do so, so be it. As always, trust your intuition. If Black Hawk or any other Native American spirit makes a connection with you, simply ask and listen.

(Mother) Sweet Water Spirit Guide

I have an interesting story about Sweet Water. Just like Black Hawk, I went through a similar experience when I encountered a Native American female statue. I envisioned a Native American woman who helped runaway slaves by providing food, blankets, and other supplies so that they could avoid capture as well. I placed this statue on my ancestor altar and honored her memory. This vision was later confirmed to me one day while riding the train.

I took a train one night to visit my parents and met a Native American woman from New Mexico who talked to me about her culture and food.

Coincidence? To add even more validity to this experience, when the train approached my stop, she along with several Black Indians who spoke a Native

American language in front of me, got off the train together. Again, this was confirmation to me. I named this spirit Sweet Water.

Sweet Water guides us to make decisions that align with our values, helping us feel proud of who we are when we look at ourselves in the mirror. She encourages people to do what feels right and to recognize when our body feels tense, which might signal an unwise decision, one that may bring us and/or others harm by disregarding the sacredness of all life.

She teaches us to practice what we preach, to take our own advice, and to avoid passing judgment on others. Sweet Water reminds us to accept that everyone's path is different, and that they are doing what they think is best for themselves, just like we are striving to do what is best for ourselves.

Sweet Water reminds us that spirituality is not about attending a place of worship or setting aside a specific time to meditate and pray. It is about staying connected to the Divine on a daily basis, by being forever grateful day and night, following your intuition, and spiritually growing by taking responsibility for our choices. She urges us to see every negative experience as an opportunity to grow.

Even when our decisions don't net the outcomes, we immediately desire, Sweet Water assures us that when we have undivided faith and stay on course, a different option and usually a better one will bring us the desires that align with our hearts and will present itself to us.

In this way, Sweet Water protects our spiritual integrity, so that our spiritual defenses remain strong.

Mythical Aakhu

Mythical aakhu are ancestral spirits whose true origins have been lost. They are remembered and honored as folk heroes and heroines. The most common mythical aakhu are the biblical characters like Moses, Abraham, and King Solomon. Other mythical aakhu are Brer Rabbit, John the Conqueror, etc.

Most mythical aakhu are the inspiration for historical aakhu, and because their true histories have been lost over time, they are typically absorbed and worked with alongside the netcharu.

Teaching Aakhu

Teaching Aakhu are ancestral spirits who most likely are not related to us by blood but have taken a liking to us because of shared interests, hobbies, occupations, careers, or goals. Most teaching aakhu are usually from other cultures and are honored because of their contributions to a particular field of interest.

For instance, those interested in mathematics and the sciences might honor Albert Einstein as a teaching aakhu. Teaching aakhu are found everywhere and can be called upon for assistance.

You can even call upon the deceased founders of the company you work for in hopes of them helping you to get a promotion or raise. Similarly, a recently deceased council member could be petitioned for assistance in helping to grease the hands of local government officials for a new project you want to begin. The options are limitless.

The Aapepu: The Misguided and Confused Ancestral Spirits

Set – While not considered a netcharu per se, Set is recognized as humanity's adversary. His number is 10, which symbolizes he 1 separated from the whole (0). Set is the lord of chaos, confusion and calamity. He is the personification of our lower self or ego and manifests as arguments, maliciousness, selfishness, and violence. As a cosmic force, Set is seen as storms, tornadoes, and dangerous winds.

It is important to understand that Set is not the epitome of evil and should not be feared. He represents our lower and tumultuous self. There are times you may have to confront him and ask why he is causing problems. He will answer, because Set, which is the personification of our subconscious, is like a child that is brutally honest with no filters.

The spirits that fall under Set's influence are called the aapepu. These are our inner demons, closely associated with our subconscious, and are not necessarily evil. However, due to unwise decisions and bad choices they made when they were alive, usually when they are around you will feel creepy like someone is watching you or that your hair is standing up on your head and the back of your neck.

In addition to netcharu (guardian spirits) and aakhu (ancestral spirits and spirit guides), we also have aapepu spirits, which are malicious, negative, confused, lowly, and misguided ancestral spirits, better known as our "inner demons." These earthbound spirits attach themselves to us usually through some type of trauma. As a result, the aapepu become the causes of us feeling angry, anxious, depressed, frustrated, etc. For this reason, in the past, these spirits were simply called "the blues."

It should be understood that generally speaking, these spirits are not inherently evil, when they were physically alive, they made unwise choices and decisions, which eventually resulted in people around them being harmed, and so the same occurs in death.

If the problems caused by aapepu are not addressed early, the spiritual consequences can lead to accidents, major losses, debilitating illness, financial ruins, substance abuse, suicidal tendencies, and violence.

How to Build a Het Aakhu (Kemetic Shaman Ancestor Altar)

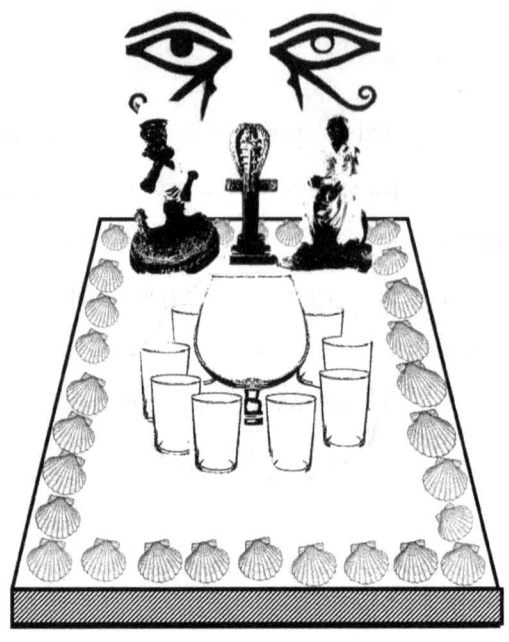

Before we go into the details on how to erect this altar, please note that I have erected the basic ancestor altar prior to building this one. Over the years, my ancestor altar evolved, growing in complexity, and I interpreted it to mean that my ancestors and spirit guides recommended it. I share this so that you do not feel obligated to build this exact altar. Remember, your ancestors and spirit guides do not have a physical body and can see things that you cannot, which includes your spiritual progress. If it is meant for you to walk down this path and erect this type of altar, your ancestors and spirit guides will let you know.

If you are reading this part of the book and feel drawn to erecting this altar, it is likely because you have an ancestor(s) within your bloodline that is inclined to help you and perhaps someone who was a magician, psychic, spiritual healer, or shaman. The way to acknowledge these ancestor(s) or spirit guide(s) is to start by venerating them and making an offering to contact them.

It should be noted that working with the spirits of the dead is not for everyone. Some people believe it is best that spirits are left alone. However, I must remind you that this is how Kemet became a powerful society. Many of the ancient edifices are memorials dedicated to the dead. If you decide to work with the spirits of the dead, understand that it is a rewarding and enlightening experience. You will learn that, although we live in a Setian society that encourages us to seek riches by adopting the western "Me, Myself, I" mindset, through this spiritual practice you will learn that no one is an island.

Through working with your spirits, you will soon discover that all those times when you felt "lucky" were likely your spirits opening doors to blessings and closing doors to dangerous and harmful paths. As stated before, the Creator does not take sides and is practically impartial. This means that it is in our best interest that we venerate our spirits because they are your personal allies, always looking out for you.

A het aakhu literally means "house ancestors." It is a resting place for your ancestral spirits and spirit guides. Aside from venerating the aakhu, the purpose of honoring the spirits using the het aakhu is for them to share their wisdom and help in resolving issues regarding family health, family protection, family property, conflicts within the family, breaches of ethics within the family, assistance with irrational or irresponsible behaviors, and addictions. These spirits are the guardians of family affairs, traditions, ethics, and morality.

Therefore, what you will need to build a Kemetic Shaman Ancestor Altar (Het Aakhu) are:

- Small table, bookshelf, dresser, or box that is large enough for photos and heirlooms to be placed upon.
- Photos and heirlooms for your deceased.
- White seashells or white rocks (at least four, but preferably more).
- Frankincense, frankincense and myrrh, or sandalwood incense.
- One white crucifix, ankh, or a pair of Eyes of Ra to symbolize the sign of the Divine. (optional).
- One large clear glass goblet for water.
- Eight clear glasses for water.
- One white tablecloth or white covering.
- One white candle.
- A dozen white or yellow flowers (optional).
- A small glass bowl for perfumes and colognes.
- A glass ashtray.
- A shot glass for liquor (e.g., rum, vodka, gin, etc.).
- One white coffee cup.
- Offerings such as cigars, cigarettes, liquor, fresh fruit (e.g., apples, oranges), or spirit money (optional).

Before we begin, I have to apologize if I sound a little preachy. I must state this: There are a lot of people who approach this practice with rigid rules in regard to how to erect, set up and perform rites on the bóveda, but these people are following a religious mindset and ritual. From this perspective, they are approaching our spirits from a Western mindset, which is an entity that exists outside of us to be worshiped or feared. The reason I refuse to use certain prayer books is because they are written from this perspective and depict human beings as being sinned, flawed, and subordinates to the spirits. This is the wrong mindset in my opinion. Our spirits are supposed to be our allies. While negatives exist, so do negative people. The same way you avoid negative people is the same way you avoid negative spirits. Focus your practice on spiritual empowerment, and you will very rarely encounter negative spirits. When you do encounter negative spirits, you will be prepared and know how to protect yourself and your home of them.

This type of altar is popular particularly among those who are Kongo descendants because it strictly follows your intuition. You basically add or subtract items off the altar as you feel inspired to do so. It is truly a natural process and there is nothing difficult about it.

To build a het aakhu, there are only three ironclad rules you must follow and they are:
1) Attend to your het aakhu faithfully, which means once a week change the water and give them candles. Please do not leave burning candles unattended.
2) Do not allow your het aakhu to fall into disarray, meaning do not leave decaying flowers, food, etc. on the altar.
3) Never put an image of a living person on the het aakhu.

Now, let's build the altar step-by-step:
Using a mild soap detergent, clean the table, bookshelf or box of physical debris. Allow to air-dry, then place a white tablecloth on top of it, which symbolizes Osar's purity and the bone memory of all our ancestors who came before us.

1) Scour the white seashells or white rocks with salt which is used to repel spirits. Then, thoroughly rinse off the salt. Use these to create a spiritual border around the edge of the altar to mark where the spiritual and physical realm meet.

2) Place the crucifix, ankh, or the Eyes of Ra in the center of the het to symbolize Maa.

3) Place photos of your masculine ancestors on the left-hand side to represent Shu, the Kemetic yang energy or fire spirits. Then, place on the right-side photos of your feminine ancestors to represent Tefnut, the Kemetic yin energy or water spirits.

4) Place one large glass goblet in the center of the het and arrange eight smaller glasses around it. These nine glasses symbolize the nine major spiritual forces, clans, cycles, the gestation period, the nine divisions, and the nine guardian spirits that govern your ancestors.

5) Add a white candle on the flat surface of the altar. You can also make offerings to your ancestors and spirit guides by placing flowers, black coffee with no sugar (for alertness), cigars, cigarettes, a small bowl for colognes and perfumes, etc. If you offer food, make sure that it does not have any salt in it because salt repels spirits.

Once your altar is set up, there are two main rituals that you can use to honor your aakhu using the het aakhu.

General Weekly Ritual:

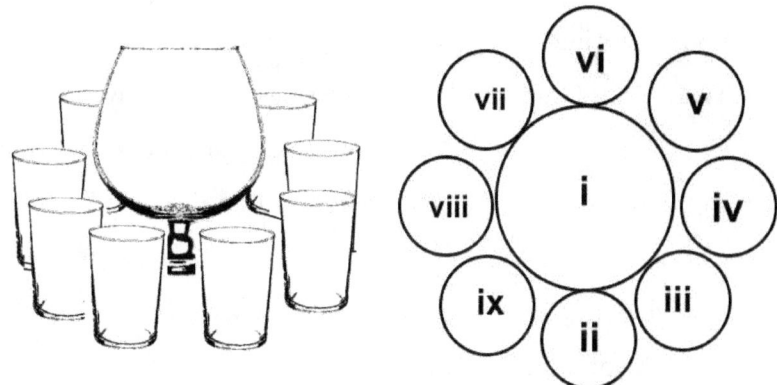

This is a simple ritual that is good to use when you don't have a lot of time to honor your aakhu.

1. Light your incense, then approach the altar. Start by knocking three times.
2. Since your Higher Self is symbolized as your Osar, say a prayer in your own language, giving thanks and praise to the Divine for all of your blessings.
   a. It is a common practice to recite the Lord's Prayer or Psalm 23 within the African American and Afro-Latino communities because they are very powerful prayers. I personally like to use the Lord's Prayer because when I say, "Our Father," I identify with Hru speaking to his father Osar (my Higher Self), who is also our first deified ancestor.
   b. Majority of the Psalms can be used in this manner as well. Note, the significance of this mental practice is to reprogram our minds to identify with being made in the image of the Divine, rather than seeing ourselves as sinned and flawed creations of God.

3. Say a prayer asking that the Divine bless, strengthen, and enlighten all of your aakhu, known and unknown.
4. Pour water into the glasses.
5. Thank your Osar for all of the blessings that you have in your life.
6. Call upon your Osar to bless your aakhu (ancestors and spirit guides) with strength, wisdom, and energy so that they will be able to assist you.
7. State the offerings you are giving to your aakhu.
8. Place the offerings on the het.
9. Petition your aakhu to assist with any issues you might be facing.
10. Afterward, thank your ancestors and allow the candle to burn out. Repeat this ritual next week on a day that is convenient for you.

Elaborate Weekly Ritual:

This more elaborate ritual takes a lot more time to perform but it creates a stronger mental impact and can help you connect more deeply with the spirits that are willing to assist you. For instance, while writing this manual, I experienced a candle tipping over and wax spilled on to my number five (v) glass. (Thankfully, I was nearby, which is the reason you should never burn candles unattended). I immediately did a reading and discovered that my Hru had averted some negative energy coming my way.

Here is how to perform the ritual:

1. Approach the altar as before by first lighting your incense and knocking three times, either on the altar itself or on the floor before the altar.
2. Say a prayer in your own language, giving thanks and praise to the Divine for all of your blessings.
    a. It is a common practice to recite the Lord's Prayer or Psalm 23 within the African American and Afro-Latino communities because they are very powerful prayers. I personally like to use the Lord's Prayer because when I say, "Our Father," I identify with Hru addressing his father Osar (my Higher Self), who is also our first deified ancestor.
    b. Majority of the Psalms can be used in this manner as well. This practice helps train our minds to identify with being made in the image of the Divine and not as sinned and flawed products of God.
3. Say a prayer asking that the Divine blesses, strengthens and enlightens all of your aakhu, known and unknown.
4. Pour water into the glasses in the proper sequence, saying the following statement:
    a. "I pay homage to **[Ancestor's Name]**," repeated three times.
5. State the offerings you are giving to your aakhu.
6. Place the offerings on the het aakhu.
7. Ask your aakhu to assist in any issue you might be having.

8. Now you can petition your aakhu to assist in any issue you might be having.
9. Sit at the altar as long as you like and contemplate or speak with your aakhu as you would with a trusted family member and friend. Tell them how you feel or what is troubling you, then ask for their assistance in the matter at hand.
10. Afterward, thank your ancestors and allow the candle to burn out. Remove all food offerings from the altar as soon as they begin to spoil.
    a. Ideally, you should place these offerings in the woods at the foot of a tree, but if you live in the city, it is more convenient and safer to simply dispose of the food in the trash since the spirits have already consumed the essence of the food anyway.
10. Repeat this ritual weekly on a day that is convenient for you.

i.	♃	I pay homage to the spirits of Osar. Thank you for wisdom, prosperity, peace and unity.
ii.	♄	I pay homage to the spirits of Sokar. Thank you for perfect health.
iii.	♀	I pay homage to the spirits of Nebhet. Thank you for love, peace and harmony.
iv.	♃²	I pay homage to the spirits of Maat. Thank you for balance, order and righteousness.
v.	☉	I pay homage to the spirits of Hru. Thank you for courage, power and victory over my enemies.
vi.	♂	I pay homage to the spirits of Hru Aakhuti. Thank you for protecting me from danger seen and unseen.
vii.	☿	I pay homage to the spirits of Npu for luck, better opportunities and open roads.
viii.	♃¹	I pay homage to the spirits of Djahuti. Thank you for knowledge and wisdom to resolve all problems peacefully and with ease.
ix.	☽	I pay homage to the spirits of Oset. Thank you for providing for all of my needs and protecting me and my family.

In addition, you can also honor specific aakhu you have a special connection with, such as your Papa/Uncle or Momma/Auntie spirits, along with any other spirits you feel a kinship with.

One of the main reasons that Hru was able to defeat Set was because he had formed a partnership with his ancestor, Osar. I am reminded of this partnership every time I visit my altar. Instead of just asking for my spirits to assist in a matter, I strive to form a partnership with them especially when dealing with certain matters. One of the ways to do this is through planning using the Maa Aankh.

Planning According to Divine Order

When working with the ancestors, spirit guides, or any spirit, for that matter, it is very important that you make your intentions clear. One of the best ways I have found to do this is by using the Four Ras of the Maa Aankh as a guide for writing petitions and stating your requests. This approach establishes a clear intent, defines your goals, allows you to see your spirits' participation in your project, and outlines what is physically expected on your behalf:

- Khepera (Sunrise/Birth): The Khepera corresponds to the air element and signals the beginning and the quest for knowledge. start by writing down what your current situation is and how you would like it to change. Be as specific as possible.
- Ra (Midday/Life): The Ra corresponds to the fire element and signals the need to declare one's will. Using the information from the previous step, condense it into a single sentence, statement, or phrase.
- Ra Atum (Sunset/Death): The Ra Atum corresponds to the earth element and signals death, which simply means transformation or change. Ra Atum reminds us that we cannot get what we want by doing the same thing that got us to this particular point. Therefore, we must sacrifice the old self (attitudes, behaviors, etc.), which may require getting out of your comfort zone. Here, write down the spiritual

- practices, physical activities, and any other functions that you are willing to do to change or improve your situation.
  - Amun Ra (Midnight/Rebirth): According to Kemetic belief, the physical world emerged out of the spiritual, so the Amun Ra moment corresponds to the element of water–a time of silence. List the desired results or other physical indicators that will signal progress towards your goal.

As you plan the steps necessary to manifest your goal, keep an open mind; you may have to alter your plans. The purpose of following a plan is to outline how your goal will manifest and what you need to do in conjunction with your spirits.

Simple Technique to Contact Your Spirit Guide

As I stated previously in this book, contacting your spirits has more to do with your ability to enter into a higher trance state. Higher trance states can be achieved by simply chanting or repeating declarations. In the church, people would go into a higher trance state by simply repeating "Jesus" or "Hallelujah." But honestly, any word or phrase repeated numerous times can lead you into a trance state.

For instance, to contact your aakhu, specifically your spirit guides, simply repeat, "Show me my spirit guides" or "Who are my spirit guides?" Then, clear your mind of any expectations and simply allow whatever impressions to make itself known.

Many of us, influenced by religious fervor, the horror and science fiction film industry, expect spirit communication to be dramatic, like being knocked off our ass like the biblical Paul. In my experience, when communication with spirits is dramatic, it is because the other 1,001 ways they tried to communicate went unnoticed. I honestly believe that I would not have become deathly ill if I had followed my intuition prior to the illness.

So, learn to trust your intuition. By the way, you do not need to light a candle at your het while doing this, however doing so will help you to focus on meeting them. Simply chant the phrase, request, or command until it resonates with you and quiets your mind. Then, observe the subtle impressions that come to mind.

Got Bubbles in Your Glasses?

Oftentimes, after pouring fresh water into your nine glasses, you will notice that the water starts very clear and fresh. Then, an hour or so later, there are these tiny bubbles that appear inside your glasses.

Depending on who you talk to, you will hear numerous explanations as to why these bubbles have appeared. Spirits communicate to us in the subtlest ways based upon our cognizance. In my experience, since my glasses are dedicated to specific spirits and my het aakhu (altar) was erected for spiritual development, these bubbles signify the presence of spirits associated with that particular netchar.

- o Think of these tiny bubbles as their fingerprints or proof that your ancestors and guides from a particular netchar are near. For instance:If you have tiny bubbles that appear in the top left glass (Number vii), it signifies that your Npu spirits are present.
- o If the bubbles appear at the bottom of the glass, it indicates that the spirits of the Npu come to give you a warning.

- If the bubbles appear at the top of the glass, the spirits of Npu come and bring good luck.
- If the bubbles appear in or near the center of the glass, the spirits come with wise counsel and spiritual blessing.

Note that this is different from placing a glass of water on your nightstand or under your bed while you sleep, which is a protective measure. The water is used to capture negative spirits and clear your dreams. If bubbles appear in that glass, it simply indicates that the water has captured some wayward spirits. In this case, dump the water in the toilet, wash the glass and before retiring to bed, place another cool glass of water either under your bed or on the nightstand.

For this reason, you should not leave half glasses of water around the house, especially if you honor your ancestors and spirit guides. Doing so can attract unwanted spiritual energy. These spirits will wander around in your home regardless, but we do not want them to stick around. Think of unwanted spirits as those unwelcome family members or associates who show up looking for loose change in your home. When they come around, you always have to check to make sure they didn't lift anything that was out in the open. We want these spirits, just like we want these people, to grow up, so don't leave water out.

What Do the Spirits Do With the Offerings?

No one really knows what the Spirits do with the offerings. What is known is that our aakhu do not need food, money, or any of these physical things because they do not have a physical body and, therefore, do not have physical needs. However, what our Spirits need is energy. This energy can come from our perception of them, but it is easier to make food offerings so that we do not forget them.

When the Spirits receive offerings, they use the energy from these offerings to transform their situation. Since everything that exists comes from the spiritual and trickles down into the physical, when an offering is made to any Spirit, it takes the energy from that offering and transforms it into raw energy, helping to make physical things manifest. This concept may be difficult for some of us to understand, but thankfully, you don't have to understand how it works, just that it does.

That being said, remember that our Spirits were once people too, so do not engage in a "tit for tat" with them. Meaning, do not tell your Spirits that if they assist you with X, you will give them Y. I have found that this approach often results in rushed and subpar outcomes. Instead, treat your Spirits with respect. Spend time with them, and do not only reach out to them when you are in need. When you nurture this relationship, they will gladly help you.

Additional Offerings

As I stated before, there is no definitive "right" or "wrong" way to work with your het aakhu. I always tell people that the right way is what gets us the desired results, while the wrong way is what leads us undesired results or does not work at all. This is because we are all unique, so as long as you are following the three rules stated above, you are perfectly fine to do whatever you will.

That being said, no one really knows what goes on in the spirit realm. No one knows why the spirits need food, water, drink, or even money. Yes, there are plenty of theories, but no one really knows because we are not dead. All that I know is that as you spend more time with your het aakhu, praying and lighting candles, you can ask them what additional items they might find useful, or sometimes, they will tell you directly. These requests are strange and bizarre, but I encourage you to trust your intuition. Here are a few charms you might want to include:

- To attract more positive energies into your home, try adding a drop of Florida Water to your glasses after you have poured the water.

- Place a small bowl of colognes and perfumes, in addition to Florida Water, on your het aaku to attract positive spirits. Spirits like perfume and colognes.

Saints, gods, and figurines are common items that your Spirits will ask you to place on the het aakhu. As you spend more time working with your het, Spirits will notice your dedication and want to work with you. Then, out of the blue, you will suddenly have an idea to look for something to place on your het aakhu, or something may catch your eye while you're out shopping, that you think would look nice on your het. These are all signs from your aakhu that they would like a particular item to represent them.

These items are indirectly associated with one of the netchar. However, do not assume that it means that the Spirit followed the netchar during their lifetime. These tools are often symbolic and help the aakhu to learn. For instance, one of my deceased grandfathers wanted to be placed near the door of my home, which is associated with the Kemetic messenger netchar Npu. Now, my grandfather did not practice anything close to the Kemetic religion, so I didn't initially understand why he wanted his photo moved there. After thorough investigation, I learned that it was because there was something he was struggling with, and Npu, being a psychopomp spirit, helped him. So don't be alarmed if you are inspired to place a Hindu god or goddess on your het aakhu, or even other objects like feathers.

Sometimes, your Spirits will try to get your attention by requesting offerings outside of your comfort zone. For instance, you may feel drawn to make a donation to a charity or to volunteer your time and energy to a cause. Whatever you promise to do, make sure to fulfill your promise. Spirits truly believe in appreciating what you earn. If you take something for granted or fail to honor your commitments, they may staunchly sit back and allow it to slip through your grasp.

Rituals with Spirit Money

One of the rituals that has become increasingly popular in recent years is the burning of joss paper, also called "Hell Money" or "Spirit Money." Joss paper, made from bamboo or rice, burns very quickly. In China, joss paper is used to make what is called "Hell Money," "Hell Notes," or "Spirit Money," which is printed to look like currency, such as money, gold, silver, coins, etc. This is burned as an offering to the ancestors.

The story goes that when Christian missionaries first went to China, and observed the Chinese burning money to their dead, they remarked that the ancestors must be in hell. Because ancestor veneration is not new to religious dogma, the Chinese embraced the comment to validate their belief that their ancestors were in torment and could bribe their way into higher realms.

When I first heard of this ritual practice, I was reluctant to perform it because it was not African. The spirit money I saw were big colorful pieces of paper with a Chinese god on it. But when I put my ego aside, I was reminded that the mind cannot distinguish between what is real and not real. So if I told myself that I was burning money to help my ancestors, my mind would eventually believe that the money was helping my ancestors. Later, I found some spirit money that was designed to look like American greenbacks, which I felt more relatable for my ancestors would appreciate it more.

After performing the ritual a few times, I was visited by an ancestor who had been mugged in life. This ancestor had been carrying around that energy of being victimized for a while until I decided to burn some money for them. So, I can personally attest that this ritual helps spirits who are suffering financially. I burn spirit money for two reasons:

1. As an offering.
2. As a form of payment.

As part of my weekly offerings, I give spirit money to my aakhu for sharing with me their knowledge and wisdom, for protection, guidance, peace in my home and prosperity. I offer them spirit money. Sometimes, I write notes like, "Thank you for protection, guidance, peace in my home, and prosperity." Then, I say, while the money is burning, "To my aakhu, known and unknown, I burn this money for you to use, so that you will give me money to use."

As a form of payment, the spirit realm is set up much like the physical realm. Just like things have costs in this realm, they have costs in the spiritual realm as well. Some of our ancestors may lack the resources to get what they need and may need assistance to purchase it from another spirit. The spirit money is burnt to ensure that they have enough to make these purchases.

There is a strong belief that there are a lot of ancestral spirits that exist as "hungry ghosts." These spirits are allowed to do menial tasks and will sit at the feet of the various gods, goddesses, saints, and other divine figures, assisting out of charity. These spirits are commonly known as altar spirits because they can be found in churches, sacred sites, and similar places. They help to create a spiritual atmosphere surrounding holy places and any time an altar is built; they are attracted to it. Spirit money is burned for these spirits as payment and is accepted by them because we do not know and have a rapport with them, as we do with our aakhu.

When I ask my aakhu (or any spirit for that matter) for their assistance, and since you cannot get something for nothing, I will approach the het aakhu respectfully and knock as usual. Then, I light a candle and I say a prayer asking for my spirits to help me with a specific issue. I write my request and express my gratitude on the spirit money. For example, "Thank you for helping me to maintain good health." Then, I burn the spirit money and extinguish the candle and leave, trusting that the aakhu are on the job.

How to Divine with the Ancestor Altar

The het aakhu is a remarkable, multi-purpose altar that works intuitively. This is one reason it can be found in Central and Southern Africa. Simply put, if something does not feel right to you, trust your instincts and remove those things that seem out of place.

The het aakhu can also be used as a tool for divination by "reading your glasses." Here's how:
1. Approach the altar as usual by knocking three times.
2. Light a candle.
3. Assuming you have already performed one of the weekly rituals, recite the Lord's Prayer.
4. Ask your aakhu a question.
5. Gaze into the glasses and wait for an answer.

Be aware that the answer most likely is not going to be dramatic, as portrayed in the movies, no water turning into red wine or flames shooting everywhere. But be aware that your way of getting answers might be different from what you think it should be. You may be looking for images and get feelings, or even have thoughts. It is very easy to overlook answers from our Spirits.

For additional clues on how to communicate with the ancestors, refer to *Part One: How Do Your Ancestors Communicate with Us?* For other methods of divination, see the Kemetic tablets in *Maa: A Guide to the Kamitic Way for Personal Transformation.*

When Will My Magick Work?

Over the years, I have found that certain spiritual and magickal practices manifest change faster than others. The speed depends on the beliefs that we hold in our minds. For instance, if you were raised by loving parents who worked hard, saved money, and provided food and shelter for you as a child, but more than once struggled to pay bills, you might have heard phrases like, "Money does not grow on trees." Regardless of what you think about money now and regardless of all of the books you have read about money, your subconscious believes that, "money doesn't grow on trees." This can subtly sabotage your efforts to manifest wealth quickly.

So, this belief will affect how magick manifests physical things in your life. Note that it is not impossible, but just keep in mind that certain beliefs might cause your goals to manifest slower than others. It is best to know different ways to manifest goals.

For Fast Jobs that will take 0 to 30 days: I have found that prayer, chanting of simple phrases, and simple candle magick works best. These methods are ideal for goals that do not require a lot of energy.

For Short Term Goals that will take 1 to 6 months: I have found that candle magick and onetime rituals work best. This is for goals like changing an individual's attitude or behavior.

For Spiritual Goals that will take 6 months to one year: I have found that it is best to use autosuggestions combined with visualizations because it takes on average 21 days to create a new habit and that is depending on if you are aware of the old habit. By expecting to see changes within six months to a year allows you to really focus on the change and any side effects along the way.

For Life changing Goals: These goals typically take more than a year because they involve a total change in character and personality. Therefore, when asking your aakhu for assistance, plan accordingly how to petition your Spirits and the method you will use to get the best results.

However, I must add that the best results come when you are not focusing on them.

Making A Way of Life

I hope through this discourse you see that working with your ancestors and spirit guides depends more on your mindset than on physical tools. There is nothing hard or scary about working with your ancestors and spirit guides. It is a rewarding experience if you take the time to cultivate it. In fact, it is because of working with my ancestors and spirit guides that I have a better understanding of how life functions.

I can truly say that I used to have a one-sided perspective (like most people) because we are taught to focus only on what we can assess through our physical senses. In other words, if we cannot see it, touch it, smell it, taste it or physically hear it, it does not exist. This erroneous way of thinking leads us to see life as a bunch of accidents and happenstances. Through working with my ancestors and spirit guides, I learned that everything has a cause. When we see physical events occur, technically we are witnessing the physical effects of unseen causes.

There are other things that my ancestors have helped me with such as understanding concepts like reincarnation, and much, much more, which again will expand your consciousness. To go further in this practice, I would suggest that you follow these outlined steps:
1. Always approach your het aakhu with a positive and open mindset. If at all possible, remove all electronic devices from your space so that it does not interfere with your ability to make contact with the spirit.

2. Begin to honor and work with one of your biological ancestors. Use objects that your ancestors owned like jewelry, glasses, clothing, etc. because these objects contain a small degree of their soul and can be used as tools to contact them. However, if you do not have these objects, no worries, it is all based upon your mind.

   That being said, I should also point out that you do not need to go to the graveyard. The whole point of using graveyard dirt or even visiting a cemetery is just to get you in a particular state of mind where you are open or receptive to the spirits. The same effect can be accomplished by using a simple photo or even a drawing of your ancestor.

   Keep in mind that if you do choose to go to a cemetery, you may be opening yourself up to all of the spirits that are present. It is best to communicate with one ancestor on a regular basis to get yourself acclimated with the other side. Always try to work with an ancestor before you work or try to contact an unknown spirit.

   Ideally, you should call upon an ancestor who was involved in this type of spiritual work as you. If you do not know who this ancestor(s) was, simply go to your het aakhu and state that you would like to meet the ancestor who led you to this path. Then, be patient and wait for a response. Remember, the response does not have to be dramatic, and it could come in your waking state, while talking, walking, watching TV, or while you are asleep and dreaming. It might be helpful to have a journal to write down responses as well.

3. Make sure that you light a candle and/or have water available for the spirit to draw energy from. You can also use crystals, but I would recommend using crystals only if you are familiar with the spirit whom you are contacting. Clear quartz crystal is great for communicating

with spirits because it helps to keep the energies clear and pure, but other crystals like amethyst and black obsidian are good as well.

4. When you call upon a spirit to communicate with you, you do not need to have any special invocation or prayers. Just simply say, "I call upon (fill in the name) to speak with me. Note that if the spirit you called upon does not respond, another might.

5. Usually when the spirits come, you will receive a lot of visions, memories, ideas, that you will most likely interpret to be random thoughts, but this is your spirit. Write down whatever comes to mind in your journal. Do not try to interpret the message yet, simply write it down.

6. Understand that talking to spirits is not like picking up the phone and talking to your family or friends because the Spirits have no physical body, so they communicate differently by giving you images. For this reason, remember to always verify what spirits tell you. By getting in the habit of always verifying information from spirits, you will discourage trickster aapepu from misleading you. This will also strengthen your rapport with your aakhu and other benevolent spirits willing to assist you.

7. Last, but not least, remember to have fun with this practice. Spirituality is not supposed to be boring nor is it supposed to be a chore It should be an escape from the boring, ordinary and mundane physical reality. So, have fun learning and interacting with your spirits.

Final Words

As you can see, honoring, venerating, and working with your ancestors is not difficult. In fact, it is quite fun and fascinating because a whole new world opens up to you that you may not have known existed.

The more you work with your ancestors, the more you will begin to see that the Kemetic people were not fascinated with death, as the archeologists and so-called Egyptologist often claim. The Kemetic people were spiritualists, and like contemporary spiritualists, they had insight from their ancestors on how they should live their lives. This is why Kemet became one of the longest-existing civilizations on the planet.

In this day and time, we need all of the insight that we can get because the current civilization, due to a lack of ethics and morality, is crumbling. To ensure that we do not get trapped under the falling mortar, it is in our best interest to remember and honor our ancestors.

However, our ancestors and spirit guides, much like loving parents, want us to do better than them. The last thing that our spirits want is for us to be running around worshiping them and giving them our power. They know that many of us need to feel their presence to escape the conditioned mindset that we have acquired in this lifetime. But they wish that we develop our divine abilities, which would be evident that we, as their children, are doing better than they have in truly realizing our divinity. This is what would make all of our spirits proud. If we all strive to accomplish this feat of growth and self-realization; we definitely will change the world.

Selected Bibliography & Suggested Reading

Browder, Anthony T. Nile Valley Contributions to Civilization. Institute of Karmic Guidance, 1992.

Fu-Kiau, K. Kia Bunseki. African Cosmology of the Bantu-Kongo: Principles of Life & Living. Athelia Henrietta Press, 2001.

Hollenweger, W. J. The Pentecostals: The Charismatic Movement in the Churches. Augsburg Publishing House, 1972.

Kaslow, Andrew J. and Claude F. Jacobs. The Spiritual Churches Of New Orleans: Origins, Beliefs, And Rituals Of An African American. University of Tennessee Press, 2001.

MacGaffey, Wyatt. Custom and Government in the Lower Congo. University of California Press, 1970.

MacGaffey, Wyatt. Religion and Society in Central Africa: The BaKongo of Lower Zaire. The University of Chicago Press, 1986.

Miranda and Stephen Aldhouse-Green. The Quest for the Shaman: Shape-Shifters, Sorcerers and Spirit Healers in Ancient Europe. Thames and Hudson, 2005.

Moore, Derric. Kamta: A Practical Kemetic Path for Obtaining Power. Four Sons Publications, 2011

Moore, Derric. Maa: A Guide to the Kemetic Way for Personal Transformation. Four Sons Publications, 2012

Moore, Derric. Maa Aankh: MAA AANKH: Finding God the Afro-American Spiritual Way, by Honoring the Ancestors and Guardian Spirits. Four Sons Publications, 2010

Moore, Derric. Maa Aankh: MAA AANKH: Discovering the Power of I AM Using the Shamanic Principles of Ancient Egypt for Self-Empowerment and Personal Development. Four Sons Publication, 2013

Smith, Theophus Harold. Conjuring culture: Biblical formations of black America. Oxford University Press, USA, 1994.

Thompson, Robert Farris. Flash of the Spirit: African and Afro-American Art and Philosophy. Random House, 1983.

Thompson, Robert Farris. Face of the Gods: Art and Altars of Africa and the African Americas. Prestel, 1993.

Thornton, John. Africa and Africans in the Making of the Atlantic World, 1400-1800. Cambridge University Press; 2 ed., 1998

Index

Amun Ra, 17, 116
ancestor, 1, 12, 30, 56, 59, 60, 61, 62, 64, 65, 66, 67, 68, 72, 73, 75, 76, 78, 88, 93, 100, 105, 110, 112, 115, 121, 122, 127
Anubis. *See* Npu
Auntie, 90, 91, 93, 114
Black Hawk, 90, 99, 100
dikenga dia Kongo, 14
Djahuti, 20, 21, 81, 83
Fredrick Douglass, 88
Harriet Tubman, 88
Henson, Josiah, 95, 96
Historical aakhu, 88
Hru, 21
KhepeRa, 2
La Madama. *See* Auntie
Maa Aankh, 16, 17, 18, 25, 87, 115, 135
Maa Kheru, 18
Malcolm X, 88
Mammy. *See* Auntie

Martin L. King, Jr, 88
Mythical, 102
Native American, 26, 90, 96, 97, 98, 99, 100, 101
Nebthet, 20, 58, 85
Npu, 20, 58, 78, 84, 86, 117, 118, 120
Osar, 18, 19, 20, 21, 22, 23, 24, 25, 26, 27, 65, 75, 76, 77, 80, 81, 86, 108, 110, 111, 112, 115
Oset, 19, 20, 58, 85, 86, 87
Palo Mayombe, 13, 91
Ra, 2, 15, 16, 17, 18, 20, 41, 107, 109, 115, 116
Ra Atum, 2, 17, 18, 115
Set, 19, 20, 21, 22, 24, 25, 55, 65, 77, 79, 81, 103, 115
Sweet Water, 101
Teaching, 102
Uncle, 90, 94, 95, 96, 114
yowa. *See* dikenga dia Kongo

Photo Credits

Page 19 Photos Purchased from Dreamstime.com

Page 20 Photos Purchased from Dreamstime.com

Page 21 Photos Purchased from Dreamstime.com

Page 46 Photos Purchased from Dreamstime.com

Page 74 Photo by Rolf Dietrich Brecher from Germany via Wikimedia Commons,<https://commons.wikimedia.org/wiki/File:Teje_(16425402049)_(from_right).jpg>

Page 79 Photo by Rama via Wikimedia Commons, < https://commons.wikimedia.org/wiki/File:Osiris-E_3751.jpg>

Page 80 Author unknown via Wikimedia Commons, < https://commons.wikimedia.org/wiki/File:ThothBoat.jpg>

Page 80 Photos Purchased from Dreamstime.com

Page 81 Photo by Sailko via Wikimedia Commons, <https://commons.wikimedia.org/wiki/File:Epoca_tolemaica,_statua_di_ptah-sokar-osiride,_304-30_ac_ca._02.JPG>

Page 81 Photos Purchased from Dreamstime.com

Page 82 Photo by Rama via Wikimedia Commons, <https://commons.wikimedia.org/wiki/File:Maat-E_4436-IMG_7942-white.jpg>

Page 82 Photos Purchased from Dreamstime.com

Page 82 Photo by Jeff Dahl via Wikimedia Commons, < https://commons.wikimedia.org/wiki/File:Ancient_Egypt_Wings.svg>

Page 83 Photo by Shonagon via Wikimedia Commons, <https://commons.wikimedia.org/wiki/File:Horus_%C3%A0_t%C3%AAte_de_faucon_-_Mus%C3%A9e_du_Louvre_Antiquit%C3%A9s_%C3%A9gyptiennes_E_7978.jpg>

Page 83 Photos Purchased from Dreamstime.com

Page 84 Photo by Rama via Wikimedia Commons, <https://commons.wikimedia.org/wiki/File:Nephthys_N4051_mp3h8832.jpg>

Page 85 Photo by Ineni3000 via Wikimedia Commons, < https://commons.wikimedia.org/wiki/File:Anubis-_Maske.JPG>

Page 85 Photos Purchased from Dreamstime.com

Page 86 Photo by Rama via Wikimedia Commons, <https://commons.wikimedia.org/wiki/File:Isis_lactans-N_3991-IMG_2397-gradient.jpg>

Page 94 Photo unattributed via Wikimedia Commons, < https://commons.wikimedia.org/wiki/File:Josiah_Henson_bw.jpg>

Page 102 Photos Purchased from Dreamstime.com

Other Books by the Author:

MAA AANKH Volume I: Finding God the Afro-American Spiritual Way, by Honoring the Ancestors and Guardian Spirits

Kamta: A Practical Kamitic Path for Obtaining Power

Maa: A Guide to the Kamitic Way for Personal Transformation

MAA AANKH Volume II: Discovering the Power of I AM Using the Shamanic Principles of Ancient Egypt for Self-Empowerment and Personal Development

MAA AANKH Volume III: The Kamitic Shaman Way of Working the Superconscious Mind to Improve Memory, Solve Problems Intuitively and Spiritually Grow Through the Power of the Spirits (Volume 3)

The KAMTA Primer: A Practical Shamanic Guide for using Kemetic Ritual, Magick and Spirituality for Acquiring Power

En Español

Maa Aankh Volume I: Encontrando a Dios al Modo Espiritual Afroamericano, Honrando a los Ancestros y a los Espiritus Guardianes